Sunshine Spirals

TEACHING GUIDE

for Sets 1 to 4

Heinemann

Contents

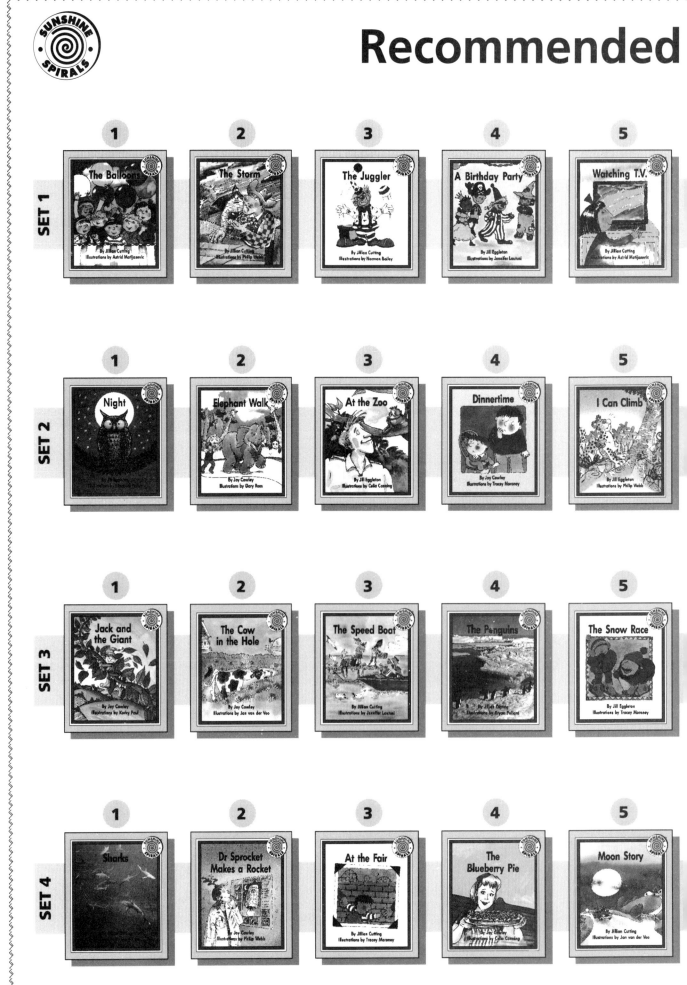

SET 1

1. The Balloons — By Jillian Cutting, Illustrations by Astrid Matijasevic
2. The Storm — By Jillian Cutting, Illustrations by Philip Webb
3. The Juggler — By Jillian Cutting, Illustrations by Norman Bailey
4. A Birthday Party — By Jill Eggleton, Illustrations by Jennifer Lautusi
5. Watching T.V. — By Jillian Cutting, Illustrations by Astrid Matijasevic

SET 2

1. Night
2. Elephant Walk — By Joy Cowley, Illustrations by Gary Rees
3. At the Zoo — By Jill Eggleton, Illustrations by Celia Canning
4. Dinnertime — By Joy Cowley, Illustrations by Tracey Moroney
5. I Can Climb — By Jill Eggleton, Illustrations by Philip Webb

SET 3

1. Jack and the Giant — By Joy Cowley, Illustrations by Korky Paul
2. The Cow in the Hole — By Joy Cowley, Illustrations by Jan van der Voo
3. The Speed Boat — By Jillian Cutting, Illustrations by Jennifer Lautusi
4. The Penguins — By Jillian Cutting, Illustrations by Bryan Pollard
5. The Snow Race — By Jill Eggleton, Illustrations by Tracey Moroney

SET 4

1. Sharks
2. Dr Sprocket Makes a Rocket — By Joy Cowley, Illustrations by Philip Webb
3. At the Fair — By Jillian Cutting, Illustrations by Tracey Moroney
4. The Blueberry Pie — By Joy Cowley, Illustrations by Celia Canning
5. Moon Story — By Jillian Cutting, Illustrations by Jan van der Voo

Reading Order

SET 1

6
The Big Race
By Joy Cowley
Illustrations by Mike Wilkin

7
Where Is My Hat?
By Jill Eggleton
Illustrations by Celia Canning

8
Where Is My Dad?
By Jillian Cutting
Illustrations by Terry Burton

9
The Dragon
By Joy Cowley
Illustrations by Norman Bailey

10
Who Ate the Bananas?
By Jillian Cutting
Illustrations by Jan van der Voo

SET 2

6
A Journey
By Jill Eggleton
Illustrations by Nick Price

7
The Space Monster
By Jillian Cutting
Illustrations by Ian McCausland

8
My Bike Can Fly!
By Joy Cowley
Illustrations by Jan van der Voo

9
By Joy Cowley
Illustrations by Elizabeth Fuller

10
The Sausage
By Jillian Cutting
Illustrations by Peter Stevenson

SET 3

6
The Sky Diver
By Jill Eggleton
Illustrations by Astrid Matijasevic

7
The Pirate
By Jill Eggleton
Illustrations by Jim Storey

8
The Magic Machine
By Joy Cowley
Illustrations by Susan Maxley

9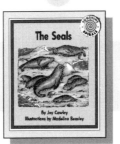
The Seals
By Joy Cowley
Illustrations by Madeline Beasley

10
The Hungry Lion
By Jillian Cutting
Illustrations by Jan van der Voo

SET 4

6
The Babysitters
By Joy Cowley
Illustrations by Val Biro

7
The Whale
By Jill Eggleton
Illustrations by Jan van der Voo

8
Grandpa's New Car
By Jill Eggleton
Illustrations by Terry Burton

9
The Magic Tree
By Jill Eggleton
Illustrations by Peter Stevenson

10
I Like Worms!
By Joy Cowley
Illustrations by Astrid Matijasevic

Sunshine Spirals
Key to Teaching Points

		Book	Sight Words	Letter/ Letter blend recognition	Focus
Set 1	1	The Balloons	the	a c m p	colours
	2	The Storm	at look the	b e l t	weather
	3	The Juggler	can I	b c j p	numbers
	4	A Birthday Party	a in with	a b p w	capital letters
	5	Watching T.V.	here is went	c g m s	story sequence
	6	The Big Race	I in is it no on the	i n o r	prediction
	7	Where Is My Hat?	a here is in on the	a f h t	question mark
	8	Where Is My Dad?	a he in is it no the	d h i n	questions
	9	The Dragon	big in is it the	g s u v	storybook language
	10	Who Ate the Bananas?	help me not said will you	d f j k l	speech marks
Set 2	1	Night	away on went	d o u w	night/day
	2	Elephant Walk	down into the went	d k l y	rhyme
	3	At the Zoo	had he his in	h s t	full stop
	4	Dinnertime	some want	b g o	food vocabulary
	5	I Can Climb	can see we	d e w	creature vocabulary
	6	A Journey	are going	l m v z	prediction
	7	The Space Monster	going is to	qu r z	space travel
	8	My Bike Can Fly!	over under	d f u	positional language
	9	The Apple	is my this	i r y	colours
	10	The Sausage	said the	revision of letters	speech marks
Set 3	1	Jack and the Giant	down went	sh	size
	2	The Cow in the Hole	get out we will	th	speech marks
	3	The Speed Boat	past went	sp	bold print
	4	The Penguins	go have what	tr	non-fiction
	5	The Snow Race	put will your	cl	healthy living
	6	The Sky Diver	down over see went	sk	positional language
	7	The Pirate	down over under up	bl sl	positional language
	8	The Magic Machine	in on put they	pl	colours
	9	The Seals	big little	sh	size
	10	The Hungry Lion	and my too	sp	ordinals
Set 4	1	Sharks	fast looked	st	sentences
	2	Dr Sprocket Makes A Rocket	from makes	bl	rhyme
	3	At the Fair	of took	sw	swimming
	4	The Blueberry Pie	did not	ch	ordinals
	5	Moon Story	there went	oo	night-time
	6	The Babysitters	after looked	cr	story endings
	7	The Whale	we will	wh	silent letters
	8	Grandpa's New Car	come had took	sl tr	sentences
	9	The Magic Tree	eat want	tr	growth and change
	10	I Like Worms!	likes play to	fr	seasons

Sunshine Spirals Teaching Guide

Introduction

Sunshine Spirals offers a confident and enjoyable start to the child who is just beginning to read. Each of the 40 books contains three short stories. The first story introduces the high frequency vocabulary (sight words) and this vocabulary is consolidated in later stories.

The Teaching Guide provides a supportive framework for the stories. It includes activities which enable teachers to prepare children for the vocabulary used in the stories, by providing oral story-tellings, and by giving suggestions on how to guide children's oral responses. It also contains many ideas of ways to extend the stories through interesting follow-up activities including early preparation for phonics.

There are 40 photocopy masters (one for each book) which help to support the important links between reading and writing. The ideas for the games and activities have been carefully researched and are both practical and simple, offering a stimulating yet structured environment in which to introduce reading.

Introducing Reading

Reading activities should build on the oral language and experiences which pupils bring from home. Teaching should cover a range of rich and stimulating texts, both fiction and non-fiction, and should ensure that pupils regularly hear stories, told or read aloud, and hear and share poetry read by the teacher and each other.
(DES/WO (1990) English in the National Curriculum)

The National Curriculum highlights the complexity of the reading process. It states what early years' teachers have always known - that reading is rarely an easily learnt skill and all children tend to put in a great deal of effort when learning to read. It is therefore essential that 'reading time' should be a time to which a child looks forward, a precious and privileged time when the child knows that he or she has the teacher's undivided attention.

Such practical considerations as a comfortable chair, good light and a relaxed atmosphere of enjoyment and support are very important. Other children must not feel that they can interrupt such sessions.

Sunshine Spirals also lends itself to small group participation and many of the activities are group based.

Early confidence comes from children who feel able to offer comments and observations about the stories they have heard and shared. As children see connections between the story contents and their own lives and experiences, they begin to make that vital connection between the print on the page and the meaning in their heads. If children are hurried into acquiring a sight vocabulary or are given isolated teaching of letter/sound relationships, then they quickly come to believe that this is what is meant by reading. They see little point in reflecting or commenting upon a story as their only aim is to get the words right.

Early acquisition of sight words and phonic knowledge are, of course, important elements in the reading process but these have to be set in a wider context which encourages children to seek meaning, information and pleasure from texts.

Reading is much more than the decoding of black marks upon a page: it is a quest for meaning and one which requires the reader to be an active participant.
(DES/WO (1989a) English for Ages 5 to 16 HMSO)

Suggested Procedure for Using Spiral Books

It is not expected that the teacher will go through every procedure with every book. However, children do need to be shown things many times and a regular and systematic approach enables children to know what to do and, through repeated success, gives them the confidence they need.

Introducing the Story

- Through questions:

  Prepare the children for the content and vocabulary of each book by asking them about their knowledge on the various topics. These questions help to focus the child's attention on to the story that follows.

- Through The Oral Story-Telling:

  In this Teaching Guide the first story in each book has an 'oral' version. This personalization of the story forms a bridge between the 'spoken words' and their written form. By 'story-telling' as opposed to 'story reading' the teacher is able to make direct contact with the child audience and so communicate the story in a very convincing way. For this reason many of the oral story-tellings pretend that the events actually happened to the teacher and this enables her or him to ask questions which encourage participation from the children, e.g. "And how do you think I felt?" Note: As the story-tellings are very simple it should be possible for the teacher to retell them without having to read them from the guide.

Book Handling Knowledge

- Show the children the cover of the book and talk about the title, e.g. "What do you think the book will be about?" "How many words are there in the title?" "How many letters are there in (one of the words)?" Show the children the author's and illustrator's names and talk about why they are on the cover of the book. Do they have a favourite author that they like to have read to them? Do they like some illustrators' drawings more than others? Use the terms cover, spine, author, illustrator, title.

- Show the children the title page of the first story.

- Show the children the contents page inside the book. Explain that every page has a number on it, starting at page one, then two and so on. Explain that these books have three short stories in them. Explain how they could use the contents page if they wanted to read or reread a particular story. See if the children can use the contents page with you by finding the final story. Praise them for achieving this difficult task. Show them other books that also have a contents page. Explain how long stories often have chapter divisions and how readers use these to help them.

- Show the children the illustrations and ask them what they think the story will be about. Show them how illustrations can help a reader to understand the story and also help the reader to build up the pictures in his or her mind.

Reading the Text

- Reading the first story.

  Read the words to the children and show them how you are reading from left to right and where you start to read on each page. Point at each word as you read it and, if possible, synchronize your voice with the word on the page.

  Read the story again and encourage the children to read it with you, letting them point to the words and show you where to start reading. Let them point at the text and echo your voice. Many children will lead the reading as they become more familiar with the text and the repetition in Spirals deliberately encourages this. In some cases the child will undoubtedly have memorized the story. This does not matter but do try to ensure that each child pays attention to the print while 'reading'.

  After reading the story ask the children some of the questions as suggested. These questions ask for both factual recall and interpretation of the story. It is important, even with very simple stories, that children are encouraged to reflect and respond to what they have read.

- Reading the second story.

  Prepare the children for the story by asking some of the questions as suggested. Encourage the child to read with you but allow and encourage the child to lead the read if possible. Praise the child for all positive actions that she or he demonstrates, e.g. knowing where to start reading, attempting the words, noticing that some of the words are the same, commenting upon the story or the illustrations.

- Reading the third story.

  Many children will manage to tackle the third story with minimal support. This story provides a consolidation of the sight words found in earlier stories or books. Do praise all attempts and allow the child to reread the stories to both his or her peers and to adults.

  It is essential that the beginning readers are not only successful but understand what it is that is making them successful. They will be using a range of strategies and these need to be made explicit to them. Too often we genuinely praise children with such expressions as "Well done!" but we do not tell them why we are pleased. If we can give the explanation to the reader then she or he will be more likely to use the appropriate strategy again, e.g. "Well done. I liked the way you left the word out and went on to the end of the sentence," or "Well done. That word does start with that sound and it was a good idea to go back and reread the whole sentence."

The Follow-up Activities

Within each book the follow-up activities cover speaking, listening, reading and writing; and each book has a photocopy master which supports one aspect of the Teaching Points.

The Focus of the Book

The focus of a particular book is highlighted at the beginning of each new book section in the Teaching Guide. In many cases the photocopy master incorporates this focus, e.g. The photocopy master in Set 1 Book 1, 'The Balloons' focuses on colours while helping children to write the sight word 'The'. Punctuation is regularly offered as a focus and in these cases it is suggested that the teacher draws attention to the punctuation when sharing the book with the group. A follow-up activity which helps to focus on punctuation is sometimes provided.

The Place of Rhyming

Many of the suggestions include either simple repetitive rhymes or activities which encourage the children to pay attention to rhyme. The work of Bradley and Bryant has shown how important it is for children to pay attention to rhyme and how they can acquire this awareness through teaching (Bradley, L. & Bryant, P.E. 1983. 'Categorizing sounds & learning to read - a causal connection', *Nature* 301: 419-21).

Letter Recognition

Some form of letter recognition is also included with each book. Research has shown that when letters are learnt within the context of making sense of the printed word it can help many children with reading and writing (Adams, M.J. 1990 *Beginning to Read* M.I.T. Press).

Sight Words

These are highlighted for the teacher at the beginning of the section for each book. Sight words are the words which are repeated as often as possible without overpowering the story. These words should not be read in isolation. The child should read the complete story before consolidating the sight vocabulary through the simple games and writing activities suggested in the Teaching Guide. If a child does not seem to be able to cope with an activity then simplify it by, say, reducing the number of words, e.g. Many children can play 'Snap' with six or more words but some will need just two or three to start with. Some children may not even be able to manage two or three. They may need matching activities. It is only through success that the child's confidence grows and it is necessary to match the level of the activity with the level of the child's ability.

Link between Reading and Writing

The links between reading and writing are very strong. Children use the books they read as a model for their own writing and, through their attempts to 'write' the words they have read they not only consolidate the vocabulary of the sight words but they come to internalize story form. Many of the photocopy masters (a selection of which are available in the form of two Activity Books, A and B) provide a framework which ensures that the child has the confidence to write. As this confidence grows children should be encouraged to try to write on their own. This might mean persuading them to try to write a word without copying it, or even to attempt to write it without having seen a model.

Recording and Assessment

Taking a Running Record

A Running Record is an accurate record of exactly how a child performs an oral reading. Each word read is marked and categorized. A more detailed form of Running Record (called Miscue Analysis) was devised by K. Y. Goodman (Goodman, Y.M. and Burke, C.L. 1972. *Reading Miscue Inventory: Manual: Procedure for Diagnosis & Evaluation.* Macmillan, London). This procedure not only marks and categorizes the words read but also groups the errors into semantic, syntactic or graphophonic miscues. This provides further diagnostic information for the teacher.

While it is possible to use a tape recorder to record a child once or twice a term on to tape which can be analysed later, this is not always practical. It is also possible for the teacher to diagnose strategies while the child is reading. However if the child finds this an obvious distraction then the results are unlikely to be really informative. The solution might be to familiarize children with the procedure so that they are less likely to find it a distraction.

There are three main ways children grapple with an unfamiliar word: they may guess by using the clues in the story line to help them; they may analyse the word, looking for sections that they recognize; or they may sound it out. Keeping a record of what children do and then helping them to use a more effective strategy is essential in order both to support them and to ensure that they make good progress.

The record sheets at the back of this book (p.171–6) can be photocopied for each child. There are records for two of the books in each of the four sets of Spirals, and records for letter and word recognition.

Marking the Text

- For every word read correctly put a diagonal stroke over it. The temptation may be to mark only when the child appears to have a problem but this indicates to the child that something is not correct and may disturb the child's reading.

- Write the letter 'T' over any word that you have to tell the child but do allow enough time for the child to tackle the word.

- If a child tries to sound out the word phonically write the sounds above the word.

- If the child makes an incorrect attempt write down the attempt above the word.

- If a child omits a word write the letter 'O' above the word.

- If a child makes an error and then self corrects write 'SC' next to the word.

- Record the information under the correct heading.

Interpreting the Record

Look at the columns and see which has the most marks in it.

Omission Perhaps the child is trying to read too fast. Decide if this is the case and talk about reading carefully. Tape the reader and both listen to the reading. Encourage the child to read on to tape for other children. Perhaps the child is trying to read on to the end of the sentence. Discuss with the child why he or she is leaving out words.

Telling If you are having to tell the reader words and no apparent attempt is being made to identify the words perhaps the book is too difficult. Help the child to think about likely words. Help the child to go back and read up to the word again. Check that the child knows initial letter sounds.

Sounding out If this interrupts the reading extensively it may be because the book is too difficult. Talk to the child about when to use this strategy. Persuade the child to try to make sure the reading makes sense. Sounding out too often can make one forget what the story is about. Read the story to the child before he or she reads to you and observe what the child does. Offer alternative strategies for the child to try before using sounds, e.g. reading the sentence again, or reading beyond the difficult word.

Self correcting This can be indicative of a confident reader where the child is aware of something that does not make sense. This strategy should be encouraged. However sometimes the child goes back to the place where the meaning was lost, and in the rereading continues to make the mistake. In this case offer the child the correct word and check that the sentence meaning has been retained. Talk to the child about strategies which might be used to access the word.

Letter and Word Recognition Records

The two record sheets provided at the back of this book (p.175 and p.176) enable the teacher to record a child's ability to recognize letters and sight words.

Make a photocopy for each child and record on the sheet on p.175 whether the child knows the sound, the name, and can write each letter of the alphabet. Similarly tick the sight words when the child can recognize them. This sheet can be completed by the time the child has read the first two sets of Sunshine Spirals.

The sheet on p.176 is for recording whether the child knows the letter blend sounds, remembers the sight words learned in Sunshine Spirals Sets 1 and 2 and records the knowledge of new words introduced in Sets 3 and 4.

Observation Records

In the reception classes it is often useful to keep a record not only of how well a child is progressing with reading but also of what knowledge a child brings to school about reading, and that child's attitude to reading.

Children who have not been introduced to the world of books before they come to school are often making great strides in their learning which go unrecognized because other children come with this knowledge so well established. Dating and recording this learning helps teachers to appreciate the progress all children are making and also reminds teachers of where a child has come from as well as where the child has got to. The following is not exhaustive or prescriptive. Teachers need to select from it things they consider worth recording.

Does the child: hold a book the right way up?

knowhow to turn the pages?

know the direction of the print?

know that reading proceeds from line to line?

know the concepts of word, letter, gap, illustration, page, full stops, sentence, author, title, contents?

read text, or pictures, or both?

Does the child: bring books to an adult and ask to have them read?

want to read or share books?

sit quietly and look at a book?

ask to take books home?

indicate that she or he likes books?

make comments about books she or he has heard or read?

attempt to retell a story she or he liked to others?

analogize from his or her own experience, relating it to something from a book?

enjoy browsing in the book corner or the library?

believe she or he is a reader?

Can the child: choose a book with confidence?

talk about stories to others?

remember stories heard or read?

predict what might happen in a story?

Spirals and Reading at Home

The inclusion of three stories within one book has the advantage of arming children with a sight vocabulary which will enable them to read a new story within the book. The child could share the first story with the teacher, practise the second story with the teacher or a friend and take home the third story to 'shine' in front of parents or guardians. So often children have either to take home a book that they have finished at school and which they do not necessarily wish to reread immediately to the adult at home or they take a 'new' book which has within it vocabulary the child has not met before and which can cause problems if the parent does not know how to help.

The Recommended Reading Order

The books have been given a suggested reading order but this is not meant to be rigid. The books are lightly graded. The first ten titles offer simple text which increases very gradually until Set 4 which contains a greater number of sentences and more complex plots. A very important aspect of reading is for children to learn how to choose books for themselves. It is hoped that children will select from Spirals not only books they know they can read but also ones which reflect their own personal interests.

Links with Other Sunshine Books

Spirals have been written to be read alongside the Sunshine readers. There is an obvious overlap in both vocabulary and style so that the child can move easily between the two strands. For instance for some children the real interest in books comes not from stories but from non-fiction. The introduction of non-fiction texts in Spirals can be supported and extended for these children by the extensive collection of non-fiction science, history and geography provided in the Sunshine titles.

The Balloons

Teaching Points for Set 1 Book 1:	sight word - the letter recognition - a c m p focus - colours parts of the body

The Balloons

Introducing the Story

Before reading the story ask the children :

Have you ever had a balloon?

When did you have it?

What colour was it?

What happened to it?

The Oral Story-Telling

One day six children I know were each given a balloon. Each balloon was a different colour.

The first little boy had a red balloon. He blew as hard as he could and made a beautiful big balloon. Then a little girl blew up her white balloon. She blew and blew as hard as she could and she made a beautiful big balloon. Next another girl blew up her green balloon. She blew and blew as hard as she could and her balloon was bigger than the others. Then a little boy blew up his blue balloon. He blew and blew as hard as he could and his balloon was very big. Then another little girl blew up her orange balloon. She blew and blew and blew and blew as hard as she could and her balloon was bigger than the others.

The last little boy looked at all the other balloons. He said, "I am going to make the biggest balloon." So he blew and he blew and he blew and he BLEW and what do you think happened to his yellow balloon?

Showing the Story

See Introduction: Book Handling Knowledge, p.8.

- Talk about the cover and together count the balloons and the children.
- Check that the children can identify all the colours.

Reading the Text

See Introduction: Reading the Text, p.8.

Talking about the Story

Some questions to ask :

Why did the biggest balloon go bang?

What do you think the other children said?

What do you think the other children did?

Follow-up Activities

- Write and colour. See the photocopy master 1 (Activity Book A1). Make sure the children start the letters at the right place.
- Bring in three balloons of different colours. Talk about the colours. Blow up the balloons. Ask the children to point at or name something the same colour as one of the balloons. Write the colours on the board. Make a tally for each colour of the things the children name. Count up the marks and talk about the 'winning' colour.
- Riddle.

  The teacher tells the group, "I can see something the same colour as the red balloon." The children have to guess what he or she can see.

Variation : The children have to say what colour they can see and the teacher must guess what it is.

• Rhyme.

The teacher says "I am thinking of a colour which **rhymes** with.....":

bed/said/head/shed	**red**
night/right/fight/sight	**white**
clean/seen/bean/mean	**green**
shoe/two/new/who	**blue**
hello/fellow/bellow	**yellow**
sink/blink/drink/wink	**pink**
sack/Jack/pack/back	**black**
town/clown/crown/down	**brown**

The Dinosaur

Introducing the Story

Before reading the story ask the children :

Do you know the names of any dinosaurs?

Could you visit a dinosaur in a zoo? If not, why not?

How big do you think the largest dinosaur might have been? As big as a car? As big as a coach? As big as a house?

Did dinosaurs have big teeth?

What did dinosaurs eat?

Reading the Text

• Show the children the title and ask them how many words are in the title. Talk about the picture. What can they see? Look at each picture in turn and then draw attention to the words on the page.

• On p.14 and 15 cover the text and ask the children what they think the words will be?

Guide incorrect answers, e.g.If the child offers, "The eyes," reply, "Yes we can see the eyes but we can see more than just the eyes."

• Before turning to p.16 ask the children to recall all the parts of the animal they have seen and ask them to predict what animal is on the next page.

Talking about the Story

Some questions to ask :

Does anyone know the name of this kind of dinosaur? (Brachiosaurus, Cetiosaurus, Apatosaurus or Brontosaurus, Diplodocus)

What food do you think this dinosaur would eat? (leaves and plants)

How big do you think it was? (20-30 metres)

How big do you think the footprints were? (Accept any reasonable answer.)

Follow-up Activities

• Game : Play "Simon says" which names parts of the body.

• Riddle : "What am I?"

I have four legs.
I have a long tail.
I live in a stable.
People ride on me.
What am I?

I have two legs.
I like to eat seeds.
I have a sharp beak.
I have feathers.
What am I?

I have no legs.
I have a strong tail.
I have two fins.
I live in the water.
What am I?

I have four long legs.
I live in Africa.
I have a very long neck.
I am very tall.
What am I?

• Rhyme : Say this poem to children and encourage them to learn it off by heart.

I wish I could see a dinosaur.
I wish there was one in a zoo.
I've lots to ask a dinosaur.
I bet that you have too.

I'd like to ask a dinosaur
About its powerful tail.
I'd ask about its size as well
It's bigger than a whale.

I wish I could see a dinosaur
See its footprints in the ground.
You see, I like dinosaurs
And I wish they were still around.

The Fancy-dress Party

Introducing the Story

Before reading the story ask the children:

Have you ever been to a party?

What did you wear?

What did you eat?

What games did you play?

The Oral Story-Telling

One day six children I knew were invited to a fancy-dress party.

One girl dressed up as a princess. What do you think she wore? She said "My dress is very pretty." One boy dressed up as a monster. What do you think he wore? "He said, "My teeth are sharp." One boy dressed up as a pirate. What do you think he wore? He said, "My dagger is very sharp." One girl went dressed as an astronaut. What do you think she wore? She said,"My helmet is very big." One boy dressed up as a cowboy. What do you think he wore? He said,"My hat is very big."

The last child dressed up as a ghost. What do you think she wore? And what do you think she said to make all the other children jump?

Reading the Text

• Show the children the title.

• Encourage them to read the words with you. Ask them to point at each word as they say it.

Talking about the Story

Some questions to ask :

Which costume did you like best?

What other fancy-dress costumes could you wear to a party?

Why do you think that the children were frightened by the ghost?

Follow-up Activities

• Alliterative sentences: Make up sentences (or use the ones suggested below).

Select one or two and say the sentence to the group.

A pretty princess in a pink party dress.

A munching monster met a merry mouse.

A proud pirate had a pretty parrot.

Annie the astronaut likes apples and ants.

Colin the cowboy can count cabbages.

Ask the children to join in and say the sentence with you. Ask the children if they can hear the sound of the repeated letter sound, e.g. "Can you hear the 'p' sound in 'A pretty princess ...'.

• Write the letter 'a', 'c', 'm' or 'p' and ask the children to say that sound when you put your finger on it.

• Ask the children to draw the letter in the air with their index fingers.

• Game : "Copy the letter."

Number of players : Two to six

What you need :

A strip of paper for each player containing three out of the possible four letters drawn in highlighter pen (a, c, m, p).

A pencil for each child.

Four cards, one for each letter.

What you do:

Give each child a letter strip. Shuffle the call cards. Turn over the top card and show it to the children. Ensure that all players can see the card clearly. Put the card face down on the table. Ask the players to look at their strips and write the letter in the highlight if it is on their strip. Continue until one player has filled in the three letters on his or her strip.

Letter shapes

A a

C c

M m

P p

Name_____

Write and colour

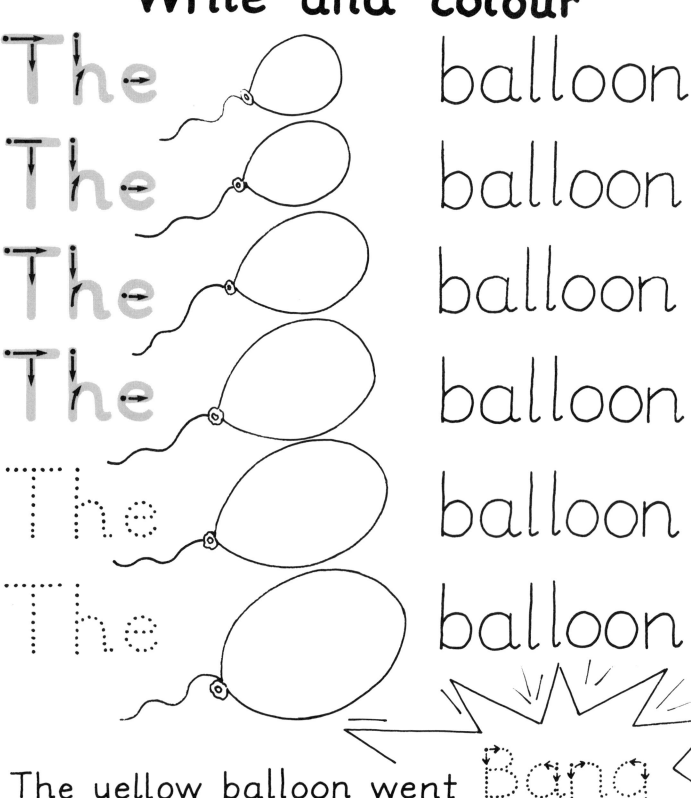

The   balloon

The   balloon

The   balloon

The   balloon

The   balloon

The   balloon

The yellow balloon went Bang

Write the words within the outline, then by
joining the dots. Then colour the balloons.

The Storm

Teaching Points for Set 1 Book 2:

sight words - at look the
letter recognition - b e l t
focus - weather
      colours

The Storm

Introducing the Story

Before reading the story ask the children:

What is the weather like today?

How do you know if it is going to rain?

Have you ever seen lightning or heard thunder?

What did you do?

The Oral Story-Telling

One day a farmer woke up very early. He looked out of the window.

There were big black clouds racing across the sky.

"Oh dear," he said to himself, "It looks as though there is a storm on the way. I must make sure all my animals are safe inside," he said.

Then he remembered. The cows were safe inside the cowshed, the chickens were safe inside the hen house and Spotty, the dog, was safe inside the kitchen.

As the farmer got dressed the wind began to blow even harder and lightning flashed across the sky. The farmer said, "I'm glad I'm not out in the storm."

Just then he remembered that Clover, his horse was still in the field.

"I must go and get him," said the farmer. "He won't like being out in the storm."

So the farmer put on his big boots and he put on his big hat and he went out into the storm. The lightning flashed and the thunder crashed and poor Clover was frightened.

"Come here," said the farmer and he held Clover's rein and led him into the barn.

"Now we are all safe inside," said the farmer and he went to get his breakfast.

Reading the Text

See Introduction: Reading the Text, p.8

Talking about the Story

Some questions to ask:

How did the farmer know that a storm was coming?

Why was Clover frightened?

Why do you think the farmer forgot about Clover?

What do you think the farmer said when he got inside the barn?

Follow-up Activities

• The group or class sing, "I hear thunder." (You may like to put actions to this song, e.g. clap after the word thunder, put your hand to your ear to hear the thunder, wiggle your fingers like rain drops and shiver when you are wet through.)

I hear thunder
I hear thunder.
Hark don't you?
Hark don't you?
Pitter patter rain drops,
Pitter patter rain drops
I'm wet through,
So are you.

- Say the poem, "Five little leaves so bright and gay."

  Five little leaves so bright and gay
  Were dancing about on a tree one day.
  The wind came blowing through the town
  Oooooo... ooooooo... ooooooo...
  One little leaf came tumbling down.

  Four little leaves so bright and gay, etc.

  (The children could use their fingers to represent the leaves and blow hard to make the sound of the wind.)

  When the children become familiar with the words ask them to take it in turns to say a line. Would any child like to try and say the whole poem to the class?

- Make a weather wheel.

  Give each child a copy of the photocopy master 2 on light card.

  Let each child colour the pictures.

  Let the child cut out the circle, helping if necessary.

  Let the child cut out the arrow.

  Fix the arrow in the centre of the chart with a split pin.

  Let the child turn the wheel to the appropriate weather condition.

Racing Cars

Introducing the Story

Picture Reading. Ask the children:

Can you name the different colours of the cars on the starting line?

Which car would you like to win the race?

How are racing cars different from ordinary cars?

Why do you think the drivers wear helmets?

Why do you think each car has a number?

Have you ever watched car racing on the T.V. or on a track?

Reading the Text

See Introduction: Reading the Text, p.8.

Follow-up Activities

- The car race.

  Find six toy cars to match the colours of those in the stories.

  Ask the children to predict which car will go furthest.

  Using a piece of stiff card angled against a thick book, let each car run down the slope under its own momentum.

  The car that travels the furthest is the winner.

- Rhyming Couplets.

  Compose some simple rhyming couplets and see if the group can supply the missing word. Here are some examples:

  We travelled far
  In Daddy's ....

  Don't be slow
  Ready, steady ....

  Look at my shoe
  Its colour is ....

  "My tractor's red,"
  The farmer ....

  I'm the winner
  Home for ....

  When he's alone
  Our dog eats his ....

- Colour dip.

  Put a selection of either tiddlywinks, multi-link cubes or small bricks into a bag. Let each child take it in turns to lift out one of the items. The child has to identify the colour and place it in a central pile of the same colour.

  When all the items have been removed the children count the number in each pile to see which colour has 'won'.

- Name the letter.

  Make four cards for each of the following letters, with a picture on one side and the letter on the other, e.g.

  t tiger teddy telephone toothbrush

  e elephant egg envelope elf

b bear book balloon bell

l lion lamb lemon lorry

Make a letter card for each letter. This needs to be large enough for all the players to see. Put the picture cards face up on the table. Hold up a letter card and say, "This is the letter 'T' and it says 't'. Can you find a picture that starts with its sound?"

Let the players pick up a card. The players turn over their card to see if their letter matches the one the teacher has. If the card is correct ask the child, "What is the name of your letter? What sound does this letter make?"

Encourage all the players to contribute to making the sound.

Select a new letter and repeat the procedure until all the cards have been removed from the table.

As the children become more confident, this could be played with the letter side uppermost. Each of the children pick up a letter to which they know the sound. They say the name of the letter and the sound it makes. They check their answer by turning over the card to check with the picture.

The Circus Parade

Introducing the Story

The aim of this story is to consolidate the sight words introduced in the previous two stories. Let the child look through the story and identify the animals.

Reading the Text

Ask the child to read the text with you. Let the child lead the reading as far as possible.

Encourage the child to take the book home and read the stories to his or her adults at home.

Follow-up Activities

• Consolidation of core vocabulary.

Make four flash cards for each of the words, 'look', 'at', 'the'

Make a sentence.

Select four objects and place them on the table e.g. book, toy, model, crayon.

Place the word cards face up on to the table.

Ask the child to select an object and then choose the words 'look', 'at', and 'the' from the table.

Finally ask each child to make a sentence, "Look at the ....," and place the object at the end. The child may like to make this into a display for the rest of the class to see.

• Match the word.

Make four flash cards for each of the words: 'look', 'at', 'the' or use the cards

from the previous game.

Turn the cards face down on to the table.

Let each player take it in turns to turn over two cards.

If they match, the player must read the word and then he or she may keep the pair.

If they do not match, the player must turn them back face down on to the table.

The winner is the player with the most pairs.

• Sing "The animals went in two by two, Hurrah! Hurrah!"

Letter shapes

B b

E e

L l

T t

Name_____

My weather chart

Today it is

Photocopy this page on to card. Colour the pictures. Cut out the circle and arrow. Fold the arrow and fix arrow to centre of chart with split pin.

The Juggler

The Juggler
By Jillian Cutting
Illustrations by Norman Bailey

Teaching Points for Set 1 Book 3	sight words - can I letter recognition - b c j p focus - numbers

---

The Juggler

Introducing the Story

Before reading the story ask the children:

Have you ever seen a juggler?

What was he or she juggling with?

Would you like to be able to juggle?

What would you use?

The juggler in the next story juggles balls. How many balls do you think he would be able to juggle?

The Oral Story-Telling

When I was little I went to a carnival. There was a juggler. Everyone wanted to see him. I was standing in the front.

The juggler threw one ball in the air. Could he catch it? Yes he could. The juggler threw two balls into the air. Could he catch them? Yes he could. The juggler threw three balls into the air. Could he catch them? Yes he could. The juggler threw four balls into the air. Could he catch them? Yes he could. The juggler through five balls into the air. Could he catch them? Yes he could. Everyone clapped very loudly.

The juggler threw six balls into the air. Could he catch them? ..... No. They all came crashing down. The juggler sat down. The balls bounced down the road.

Everyone laughed so I ran and picked up all the balls and gave them to him.

Reading the Text

See Introduction: Reading the Text, p.8.

• From p.5 onwards ask the children to tell you the number of balls the juggler is using.

• On p.7 ask the children what they think will happen. Read the story with the children. Ensure that the children point at the words as they say them with you. Note the children who are able to cope with the reversed word order on p.7.

Follow-up Activities

• Say the sentence.

Write the following letters on the board saying the name of the letter and its sound as you do: 'b', 'c', 'j', 'p'.

Say an alliterative sentence for each letter, e.g.

Jack the juggler, juggled jelly.
Bertie the bear bounced big balls beautifully.
Patsy the penguin picked purple pansies.
Cathy the camel caught a cough and a cold.

Ask the children to listen carefully to the sounds they hear in the sentences.
Can they tell you which sound is being repeated in each sentence?
See if they can point to the right letter when you say the sentence, emphasizing the sound. Let the children say the sentences and then say the name of the letter and its sound.

• Song: Sing "Peter hammers with one hammer", or sing the nursery rhyme, "1 2 3 4 5, Once I caught a fish alive".

Let the children join in with the actions of the songs.

Peter hammers with one hammer, one hammer, one hammer,
Peter hammers with one hammer all day long (Children use fist to beat time with the music on to the table).
Peter hammers with two hammers etc. (Children use two fists).
Peter hammers with three hammers.... (Children use fists plus one foot).
Peter hammers with four hammers.... (Children use two fists and two feet).
Peter hammers with five hammers.... (Children use fists and feet and nod their heads for the last hammer).
Peter's very tired now. (Children put their heads in their hands and pretend to go to sleep).

• Match the numbers.

Make circles of paper approximately 20cms diameter.

Write a number clearly in the centre of each circle.

Use objects that lock together such as Lego bricks.

Allocate a colour to each child.

Ask the children to put the correct number of their colour bricks on to each circle.

You will be able to see which children have got the right answers by looking at the colours.

Painting a Picture

Introducing the Story

Before showing the children the story ask the children:

What do you think the little girl painted in her picture?

Do you like painting or drawing?

What do you like to paint?

Talking about the Story

Tell the children the girl is painting a picture of the countryside. Ask them to guess what she is painting. Give them clues as to what she does.

She is going to paint a picture of the countryside. Is she going to paint lots of buildings and cars?

First she painted something that was big and high and that you could climb. What do you think she painted?

Next she painted something long and winding that fish can live in. What colour do you think she painted the river?

At the top of her picture she painted the sky but she decided it wasn't a sunny day so she painted some things that were big and white and fluffy. What were they?

Next she painted some things beside the river. They were tall and brown and green. What do you think they were?

In a field by the river she painted some black and white animals. These animals give us milk. What do you think she painted?

Last of all the little girl painted something very special. What do you think it was? Let's look and see.

Reading the Text

See Introduction: Reading the Text, p.8

Follow-up Activities

• Draw and colour. Give each child a copy of the photocopy master 3. Let each child add features to the outline of the child from p.16 of the reader, e.g. hair style, face features, clothes, colours. The drawing could be a self-portrait. Ask the children to colour their pictures.

• Say the rhyme: "What did I see?"

Encourage the children to join in with the repeated lines.

Walking through the countryside
What did I see?
High purple hills
Looking down on me.

Walking through the countryside
What did I see?
A rushing, tumbling river
Racing past me.

Walking through the countryside
What did I see?
Tall green beech trees
Standing near me.

Walking through the countryside
What did I see?
Black and white cows
Mooing at me.

Walking through the countryside
What did I see?
A little brown rabbit
Hopping past me.

Walking through the countryside
What did I see?
A place for a picnic
For you and me.

The Football Match

Introducing the Story

Before reading the story ask the children:

Have any of you played football?

Have you watched a match on the T.V.?

What teams' names do you know?

What do footballers wear? (Introduce words like boots, strip, kit, etc.)

Do you know the names of any famous footballers?

Reading the Text

For this story encourage the child to read the sight words with you without extensive preparation. Ask the child to point to each word as he or she reads it. When the child comes to a new word offer him or her a first sound clue e.g. I can r... I can thr...

Encourage the child to pay attention to the letter sound and the picture clue.

Note: This third story should have consolidated the sight vocabulary: 'I can...'

The child could be encouraged to take this book home and read it to an adult or older sibling.

Follow-up Activities

• Game: "Copy cat".

Sit the children in a circle.

The teacher performs some actions and the children are invited to copy the teacher. For example, the teacher hops and says, "I can hop."

The teacher then selects a child and says, "Can you hop?" The child then tries to copy the action and says, "I can hop." This child then selects another child and says, "Can you hop?" When each child in the group has had a turn the teacher chooses another action for the children to copy. The teacher could make this more difficult by doing more than one action, e.g. "I can hop and wave."

• Practising the letters 'b', 'c', 'j', 'p'.

Select one letter and have a letter corner.

Invite the children to put any small object that starts with the letter on to the table. Put out a small pile of letter sheets for the children to draw over when they have a few odd moments. These can be made by writing the letter with a broad highlighter pen and letting the children trace over it in pencil. More confident children may like to try and draw their own letters, but make sure they know where to start forming the letter. When a sheet is complete pin it up on the wall behind the table. Remember to refer to the table by the letter name and then link the sound to the letter name, e.g. "Would you like to put your jam on the 'J' table? Can you tell me the sound that jam begins with?"

Letter shapes

B   b

C   c

J   j

P   p

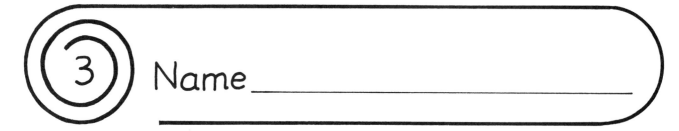

3 Name_____

Draw and colour

Add hair, face, and clothes, and then colour.

A Birthday Party

By Jill Eggleton
Illustrations by Jennifer Lautusi

Teaching Points for Set 1 Book 4:	sight words - a in with
	letter recognition - a b p w
	focus - capital letters
	storybook characters

A Birthday Party

Introducing the Story

Before reading the story ask the children :

Have you ever had a birthday party?

How old were you?

What did your friends bring?

What did you and your friends wear?

The Oral Story-Telling

I'm going to tell you a story about a special birthday party where all the children dressed up as special characters. They each had a different costume to wear. What do we call this kind of party?

The first child wore a white sheet over her head. She had holes cut for eyes, and a mouth painted on the sheet. She looked very scary. What do you think she was?

The second child came as a terrible creature that has a long tail and sharp teeth, and breathes fire. What do you think she was?

The third child decided he wanted to wear a patch over one eye, a sword at his side and a big hat with a skull and cross-bones painted on it. What do you think he was?

The next child liked to make people laugh. She wore flippy-floppy shoes, a hat with big bobbles and a round red nose. What do you think she was?

The next child wore her oldest clothes with patches on the knees. She dressed up as something that stands in the fields to frighten away the birds. What do you think she was?

There was one more child invited to the party. He wanted to be very, very scary. What fancy-dress do you think he wore?

Showing the Story

• Talk about the book title, the author and the illustrator.

• Show the children the words that make up the title of the book.

• Talk about the cover and name the fancy-dress costumes. What party game do they think the children in the story are playing?

• Show the children the title page of the first story and ask them to read the title. Can they recognize that it is the same as on the cover?

Reading the Text

See Introduction: Reading the Text, p.8.

Follow-up Activities

• Who brought what?

Ask the children, "Can you guess what present each child brought? Look at p.8. There is a ball, a piggy bank, a book, a tiger and a guitar. Who brought what?"

• Write and match. See the photocopy master 4 (Activity Book A2). Write within the lines, then joining the dots, then without help.

• Rhyme: "I'm going to a party."

I'm going to a party.
What shall I be?
I'll be a ghost.
They'll all be scared of me.

I'm going to a party.
What shall I be?
I'll be a pirate.
They'll all fight with me.

I'm going to a party.
What shall I be?
I'll be a scarecrow.
They'll all look at me.

I'm going to a party.
What shall I be?
I'll be a dragon.
They'll all hide from me.

I'm going to a party.
What shall I be?
I'll be a clown.
They'll laugh at me.

I'm going to a party.
What shall I be?
I'll be a MONSTER.
They'll all RUN from me!

The teacher can say the words of the song leaving the third line of each verse for individual children to say.

- The capital letter.

  Talk about how each letter has a capital form and a lower case form.

  The teacher could ask the group to say their names. Write on the blackboard the capital letters which start their names. Say the name of the letter in each case, e.g. "This is an 'A' and it starts Adam's name. Ask each child to say the name of the letter that starts his or her name. Show the group the capital letter 'A' that starts each sentence in this story, p.2 to p.7. Explain that we start every sentence with a capital letter. Then show the children the lower case 'a' in the same sentence.

The Picnic

Introducing the Story

Before reading the story ask the children:

Have you ever been on a picnic?

What did you eat?

Do you like picnics?

Where would you like to go for a picnic?

Oral Preparation of Vocabulary

Show the children the illustrations and ask the following questions :

Where is the boy? (If, as is likely, the children offer the answer "in the tree", point out the printed form of these words: The boy in the tree.)

Where is the girl? The woman? The man? The dog? The ants?

Reading the Text

See Introduction: Reading the Text, p.8.

Talking about the Story

Some questions to ask:

Looking back through the story can you see how the ants made their way to the picnic?

Why do you think that no one noticed the ants?

What would they do when they discovered the ant pie?

What other animals might bother you on a picnic? (flies, wasps, cows)

Follow-up Activities

- Have a classroom picnic of jam sandwiches. Let each child spread the margarine and jam on the bread and cut into small sandwiches.

- Together learn the rhyme :

  Slice, slice the bread looks nice.
  Spread, spread butter on the bread.
  On the top put jam so sweet,
  Now it's nice for us to eat.

- Do the following hand rhyme together :

  Boy in the tree says swing, swing, swing.
  (Swing arms.)
  Girl in the water says swim. swim swim.
  (Pretend swimming action.)
  Woman in the canoe says row, row, row.
  (Pretend rowing action.)
  Man in the car says go, go, go. (Pretend driving a car.)
  Dog in the basket says in my tum. (Point at tummy.)

Ants in the pie say yum, yum, yum. (Rub tummy.)

- Read the children the story of "The Giant Jam Sandwich" by John Vernon Lord (Puffin).

Bedtime

Introducing the Story

Before reading the story talk about :

Do you like going to bed?

What time do you go to bed?

What do you do before you go to bed?

Do you like having any toys in your bed?

Oral Preparation of Vocabulary

Show the children the pictures and prompt the words such as wizard and wand, e.g. "Who is in this bed?" "What is he holding?"

Reading the Text

See Introduction: Reading the Text, p.8.

Follow-up Activities

- Game: Sound Snap.

  Make cards with different pictures on them, but having letter sounds in common, e.g. sun, sock, and fish and frog.

  Shuffle the cards. Deal them out to the two players. The children each turn over a card at the same time. If the pictures start with the same sound the first child to say SNAP collects the pile.

- Song: To the tune of "Here we go round the Mulberry Bush" sing the following song :

  *This is the way we climb the stairs,
  climb the stairs, climb the stairs,
  This is the way we climb the stairs,
  before we go to bed.*

  *This is the way we brush our teeth/
  This is the way we brush our hair/
  This is the way we read a book.*

- Sending the book home.

  See Introduction: Spirals and Reading at Home, p.10.

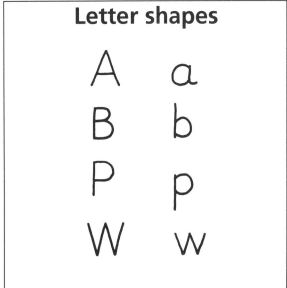

Letter shapes

Party presents

A 👻 with a ▪️

A 🎁 with a 👜

A 🤡 with a 🎸

Go over the writing and connect the silhouette to its matching gift.

Watching T.V.

Watching T.V.

By Jillian Cutting
Illustrations by Astrid Matijasevic

Teaching Points for Set 1 Book 5:

sight words - here is went
letter recognition - c g m s
focus - story sequence

Watching T.V.

Introducing the Story

Before reading the story ask the children:

Did you watch T.V. last night?

What did you watch?

What is your favourite programme?

Can you watch what you like on T.V.?

The Oral Story-Telling

Did I ever tell you about the time when my naughty little sister was extra naughty? It was in the summer and we had been playing in the garden.

My Mum called out, "It's time for bed." But my naughty little sister didn't hear my Mum because she had sneaked into the house to watch the T.V. It was a film about superwoman in space. Some monsters were attacking the astronauts. Then superwoman came to the rescue.

Just at that moment my Mum opened the door and saw my naughty little sister. "You naughty little girl, go to bed," said Mum.

What do you think my naughty little sister said?

Reading the Text

See Introduction: Reading the Text, p.8.

Talking about the Story

Some questions to ask:

Has your Mum or Dad ever turned off the T.V. and sent you to bed?

What did you say?

Follow-up Activities

• Group writing.

Tell the children they are going to make up a space story about astronauts, monsters and superwoman. You will need large sheets of scrap paper and bright felt tip pens. You are going to scribe the story that the children offer. It may be necessary to prompt the children with questions to ensure that the story stays on course, e.g. Ask the group how they would like to start the story e.g. "Would you like to start with 'Once upon a time...', 'One day...', 'There was a full moon....'?"

Let the group select the opening and then use prompting questions, e.g. "Who lived on the moon?" "Where was the astronaut going?" "What did the monster look like?" Write down the suggestions drawing attention to the writing process as you do so. At the end of the story give each child an episode to illustrate. Using large print write out the text for the group so that the appropriate text can be positioned beneath the children's illustrations.

The illustrations and text can be pasted on to art paper and simply bound to make a big book for the class. The title and the authors' names should be written on the cover.

• Join in the space song.

Children echo each line after the teacher :

Get on board the rocket
We're going to the moon
Ticket in our pocket
Be there very soon.

The stars above are shining
Twinkling in the sky
Lighting up our journey
As we travel by.

• Make a Space wall display.

Let the children cut out, or draw and paint things they might see in space. Mount these on to sheets of black paper and label.

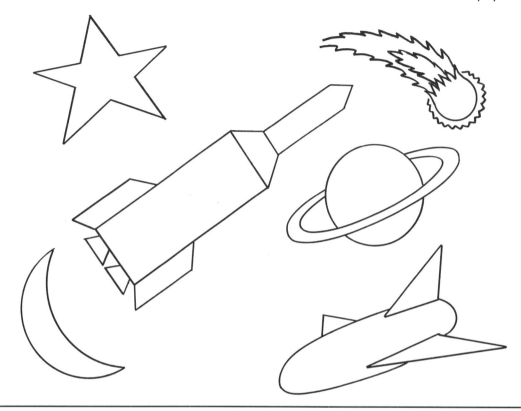

The Birthday Cake

Introducing the Story

Before reading the story to the children ask :

What are cakes made from?

What sort of cakes do you like best?

What sort of special cakes are there?

Oral Preparation of Vocabulary

Show the children the story, "The Birthday Cake". Count the candles on the cake. Prompt the vocabulary of the nouns by asking the children what each child in the story is saying, e.g."Here is the ....". Children look at the picture and guess the nouns.

Reading the Text

See Introduction: Reading the Text, p.8.

Follow-up Activities

• Memory Game.

Take a deep bowl into the classroom. Select 6 small objects e.g. die, Lego brick, rubber, etc. Show the group each object before it is placed in the bowl. Say, "Here is the ....." Ensure that the children cannot see these objects once they are in the bowl. See how many they can remember went into the bowl.

• Give each child a copy of the photocopy master 5 (Activity Book A3). Ask the children to match the pictures to the bowl of the same letter, then practise writing the letters.

• Song: "Pat-a-cake."

Pat-a-cake, Pat-a-cake Baker's man
Bake me a cake as fast as you can.
Pat it and prick it and mark it with .....
and put it in the oven for ..... and me.

Select the starting sound of a different child's name each time you come to line three.

The Boat

Before Reading the Story

Show the children the text and the pictures. Read the word 'The' and ask the children to 'picture read' the animal that gets into the boat then read the last two words 'went in', pointing at the words as you do so. At the end of p.23 ask the children what they think happened next.

Reading the Text

Ask the child to read the sight words which are 'The', 'went' and 'in'. You read the nouns.

Follow-up Activities

• Sing "Row, row, row your boat" in a round.

Row, row, row your boat
Gently down the stream.
Merrily, merrily, merrily, merrily
Life is but a dream.

• Sink the boat.

Use a washing up bowl half full of water and place a 'boat' in it. This could be the base of a margarine tub or a simple model boat. Let the children take it in turns to place a small object into the boat, e.g. Lego bricks or plastic farmyard animals. How many objects can the boat hold before it sinks?

• Read "Mr Gumpy's Outing" by John Burningham (Picture Puffin).

• Remind the children of sensible precautions when near water.
Share with the children some information from "Be Safe: Near Water" (Franklin Watts).

• Make a paper boat.
Fold a 20cms square in half to form a rectangle.
Take each corner, along the fold and fold to the centre to form two triangles.
Fold back to flat rectangle as before. Fold up a 3 cms rectangle in front and behind. Carefully fold back the two triangles inside the 3cms rectangle and flatten to form angled front and back of boat.

Letter shapes

C   c
G   g
M   m
S   s

Paper Boat

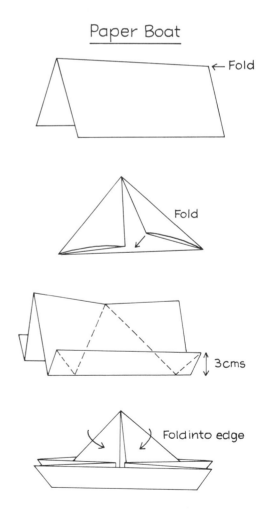

Where do the pictures go?

S _____

C _____

m _____

g _____

Connect the pictures to the bowl with the same first letter
and then practise each letter.

The Big Race

The Big Race

By Joy Cowley
Illustrations by Mike Wilkin

Teaching Points for Set 1 Book 6:	sight words - I in is it no on the
	letter recognition - i n o r
	focus - prediction

The Big Race

Introducing the Story

Before reading the story to the children share the pictures with them and ask:

Do you know what sport each of the pictures shows?

Have you ever taken part in any of these sports?

Talk about racing and ask the children:

Do you know how a race is started? (e.g. Ready, steady, go!; a flag is dropped; or a starting gun is fired)

What do people wear for different kinds of races?

Why do you think people wear helmets for some sports?

What sorts of things do people get if they win races?

The Oral Story-Telling

When I was still at school there was a big race. It was very exciting. We had to do lots of different sports in the big race. I had to ride in the big race. Then we went to a hill where I had to climb in the big race. Then we went to the water so that I could paddle in the big race. I also had to swim in the big race and then, at last, to run in the big race. Guess what happened at the end of the big race. Do you think I won?

Reading the Text

See Introduction: Reading the Text, p.8.

Follow-up Activities

• Draw attention to the sight words. Ask the children to find these words from a line of text, e.g.'I', 'in', 'the' on p.3.

• Ask the children if they can find a word that starts with the sound 'i' or 'r' on p.3, 4 and 5, etc.

• Give each child a small pile of counters. Read the story one sentence at a time and ask the children to place a counter in a line, one for each word they can hear. This activity will help children with word segmentation and it identifies for the teacher those children who are still uncertain about the concept of a word.

• Give each child a copy of the photocopy master 6 (Activity Book A4) to practise copying, and then writing without copying, the sight words 'is', 'on', 'it' and 'the'.

Letter shapes

I   i

N   n

O   o

R   r

Where Is My Skateboard?

Introducing the Story

Before reading the story ask the children:

Have you ever been on a skateboard?

How many wheels did it have?

Have you seen people doing tricks on a skateboard?

The Oral Story-Telling

Before reading the text tell the children the following story which prepares them for prediction of text. It is very important to balance the emphasis on accurate reading with an **understanding** of the story. Encouraging children to predict a text draws their attention to the meaning of the text.

One day Gran was bored. She was tired of sitting in her big arm chair. She was tired of sitting still.

She thought she would go to the shops in her car but, oh dear! the car wouldn't start. Why do you think the car wouldn't start? "Never mind," said Gran, "I'll go on my bike." But, oh dear! something was wrong with the tyres of the bike. Why do you think the bike wouldn't work? "Never mind," said Gran, "I'll go on my scooter." But, oh dear! the wheels of the scooter would not turn. What do you think was wrong with the wheels of Gran's scooter? "Never mind," said Gran, "I'll walk to the shops." But then

she saw something. It was something that had four small wheels. It had a brightly coloured board. What do you think she saw? "I will go to the shops on this," said Gran. She went to the shops. What do you think she said? What do you think the shop-keeper said? What do you think her family said when Gran got home?

Reading the Text

See Introduction: Reading the Text, p.8.

Follow-up Activities

- Game: "Hunt the thimble."

  This activity encourages children to ask questions. They have to suggest places where the hidden object might be, e.g. "Is it on the desk?" "Is it in the cupboard?" The winner chooses the next hiding place.

- Extending the story.

  Do as a group writing activity (See p.27). The teacher acts as scribe and asks the group to suggest what happens when Gran goes on her skateboard. Write the final story in large print and suggest that the children illustrate it.

- What sports are the most popular?

  Make a bar chart of the top four or five favourite sports and how many pupils enjoy each best.

My favourite sport

| Tennis | Running | Fishing | Football |

Colour in different colours for different sports

The String

Introducing the Story

Before reading the story, ask the children:

Do you like to wrap parcels with string?

What happens if you drop the ball of string?

What else unravels if you drop it?

What animal likes to play with wool or string?

Reading the Text

See Introduction: Reading the Text, p.8.

Follow-up Activities

• Clapping the tempo. Say the words from each of p.18 to 24 in turn and get the children to clap each syllable, e.g. 'String on the table' has five beats.

• Game: "Odd one out".

Read out each group of three words in turn and ask the children to identify the odd one out - the word which does not rhyme.

cat	dog	hat
book	hook	box
table	tree	key
mouse	monkey	house
carrot	parrot	picnic
clap	clock	sock
fish	friend	dish

• Game: "I spy".

Play with letters beginning with 'b', 'n', 'p', 'r'.

• The string game:

Take a length of string about 6 metres long and thread a curtain ring on to it. Tie the two ends of the string together. The group hold the string standing in a circle. One child stands in the centre with his or her eyes shut. The children pass the ring along the string from hand to hand saying the rhyme :

Pass the ring along the string
And slowly count to three
Who has the ring upon the string?
Open your eyes to see.

The child in the middle counts to three slowly then opens his or her eyes, looks at all the closed hands and guesses who has the ring.

• Make a reef knot.

Reef Knot

Right over left

1

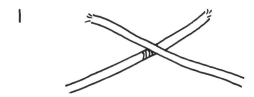

2

Left over right

3

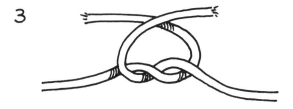

4

For joining string of the same thickness

5

Copy the word

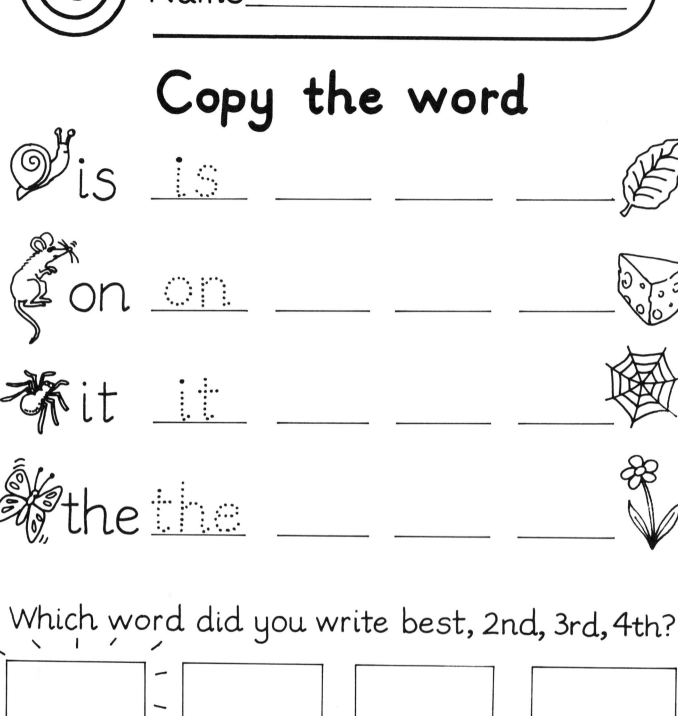

is   is _____ _____ _____

on   on _____ _____ _____

it   it _____ _____ _____

the the _____ _____ _____

Which word did you write best, 2nd, 3rd, 4th?

1st	2nd	3rd	4th

Write the words without copying.

_____ _____ _____ _____

Where Is My Hat?

Where Is My Hat?
By Jill Eggleton
Illustrations by Celia Canning

Teaching Points for Set 1 Book 7:	sight words - a here in is on the letter recognition - a f h t focus - question mark colours

Where Is My Hat?

Introducing the Story

Before reading the story, ask the children:

Have you ever lost anything?

Have you ever found anything that did not belong to you?

What did you do with it?

Have you ever hidden anything away from anyone?

The Oral Story-Telling

I'm going to tell you a story about a cheeky monkey. He belonged to my friend, Coco the clown. Coco the clown was getting dressed for the circus. He put on his big green baggy pants, and his bright spotted shirt. He painted his mouth with lots and lots of red lipstick. Then he put on his shiny red nose.

Was Coco ready for the circus? No, he was not. Where was his clown's hat? He started to look for it. He found his red sock but he couldn't find his hat. He found his red shoe but he couldn't find his hat. He found his blue sock and he found his blue shoe but he couldn't find his hat. He found his green tie but he couldn't find his hat. "Where is my hat?" said Coco the clown. Do you know who had his hat? His naughty monkey had the hat all the time. What a cheeky monkey!

Reading the Text

See Introduction: Reading the Text, p.8.

Talking about the Story

Ask the children:

What funny things did Coco wear?

What was funny about his socks?

What was funny about his shoes?

How did Coco make his face funny?

Follow-up Activities

• Song: "This clown has a funny nose."

Sing the following song to the tune of "Old Macdonald had a farm."

Mime some actions for putting on each item of clothing.

Chorus :
This clown has a funny nose
E, I, E, I, O
But what else do you think he wears?
E, I, E, I, O

Verse 1:
He has a funny hat upon his head
That is what he wears.

Chorus

Verse 2 :
He has big blue shoes upon his feet, a
funny hat upon his head,
That is what he wears.

Chorus

Verse 3 :
He has a big green tie around his neck,
big blue shoes upon his feet, a funny hat
upon his head.
That is what he wears.

Chorus

Verse 4 :
He has baggy pants that might fall down, a big green tie around his neck, big blue shoes upon his feet, a funny hat upon his head.
That is what he wears.

Chorus

Verse 5 :
He has stretchy braces that go snap, baggy pants that might fall down, a big green tie around his neck, big blue shoes upon his feet, a funny hat upon his head.
That is what he wears.

Chorus

Verse 6 :
He has bright red lipstick on his mouth, stretchy braces that go snap, baggy pants that might fall down, a big green tie around his neck, big blue shoes upon his feet, a funny hat upon his head.
That is what he wears.

- On a copy of the photocopy master 7 match the balloons to the children. The pictures in the balloon start with the same letters as those shown on the T-shirts. Colour matching balloons and T-shirts in the same colour.

- Talk about things that go in pairs : socks, shoes, gloves.

  Ask the children:

  Do you know why some things go in pairs?

- Game: Pairs

  Collect together three pairs of different socks. Place one of each pair in one box and the other three socks in another box. Two children sit back to back and pick out one sock each. They turn to see if they have made a pair. If they have, then another two children have a go. If they have not they put the odd socks back and try again.

A Kite Race

Introducing the Story

Before reading the story ask the children:

> Do you know what a kite is?
>
> Have you ever seen anyone flying a kite?
>
> How does a kite keep up in the air?
>
> How do you stop a kite flying away?

The Oral Story-Telling

When I was small I went to the park with my mum to fly my new kite. It was a windy day and lots of children were flying their kites. There was a blue kite in the sky; there was a green kite in the sky; there was a yellow kite in the sky; there was a red kite in the sky; there was a purple kite in the sky; and there was a black kite in the sky. My kite was a big yellow kite. I wanted my kite to fly the highest. I let out the string and it went up and up. My kite was high in the sky. Suddenly a gust of wind blew my kite very hard. What do you think happened? The wind blew my kite into a tree. I was very sad. But my mum shook the branch of the tree and my kite came tumbling down.

Reading the Text

See Introduction: Reading the Text, p.8.

Follow-up Activities

- Riddle: "What am I?"

  A diamond shape in the sky,
  I have no face, I have no eye
  But a tail I do possess
  Just how long you'll have to guess.
  In the clouds, birds pass me by,
  But without any wings I can fly.

  What am I?

- Make a kite collage.

  Let the children draw around templates to make a kite collage. The kite shapes can be square, box, diamond, oval, or triangle. Paste string or thread on to the kite shapes.

- If possible bring a kite into the classroom to show the children.

- Say the following rhyme :

  k is for kite flying so high,
  i is for ice cream I'd like to buy.
  t is for tree into which your kite flew
  e is for easy for me to help you.

- Sing the song, "Let's Go Fly a Kite" from "Mary Poppins".

Fishing

Introducing the Story

Before reading the story ask the children:

Have you ever been fishing?

What do fishermen catch?

What do they use to catch the fish?

Where do they sit?

What other creatures live in water? (whale, shark, crocodile, hippo, octopus)

Before pointing out the text ask the children if they can identify the creatures in the bubbles. Explain that they show what the boy **thinks** might be on the end of the fishing line. Before turning the final page ask the children to guess what is on the line.

Reading the Text

See Introduction: Reading the Text, p.8.

Follow-up Activities

- Make a fishing game.

  Draw and cut out fish shapes. Write on each fish one of the teaching point words (a here in is on the). Sellotape a paperclip to the back of each fish. Make a 'rod' from a garden cane or stick and attach a magnet to the end of the string line. Each child takes it in turn to catch a fish. If they catch a fish and can read the word they can keep the word. If not, then the fish is put back. The winner is the child with the most fish.

- Sing the song:

  One, two, three, four, five,
  Once I caught a fish alive.
  Six, seven, eight, nine, ten,
  Then I let him go again.
  Why did you let him go?
  Because he bit my finger so.
  Which finger did he bite?
  This little finger on the right.

- The question mark.

  Point out to the children the question mark at the end of each page. Explain what this symbol means.

- Pass the question.

  The children sit in a circle. The teacher asks one of them a question, e.g. "Anna, are you wearing trainers?" Anna replies, "Yes" or "No", then she asks another child the same question, "Jack are you wearing trainers?" After several children have asked and answered the question the teacher can decide on a new question, e.g. "Do you like apples?" "Have you any pets?" "What is your favourite colour?"

- Letter sounds.

  The teacher selects one of the teaching point letters ('a', 'f', 'h', 't') and says, e.g. "My name is Freddy Fish. I can only buy things that begin with my letter 'f'."

  Ask the children to 'sell' you something, e.g. football, feather, flag, flask, fog, fox.

  When a child offers an object that starts with the correct sound, reply, "Yes, Freddy Fish likes football" or, if incorrect, "Sorry Freddy Fish can't buy oranges."

  When everyone has had a go at selling things to Freddy Fish then the teacher changes the game to 'h' (Harry Horse) 'a' (Aunt Agatha) 't' (Tim Turtle).

Letter shapes

A   a

F   f

H   h

T   t

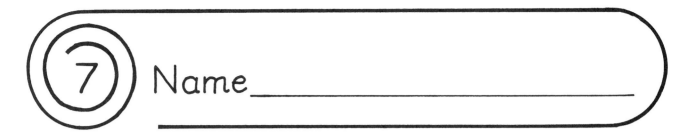

Match and colour

Match the first letter of the picture to the letter on the child's T-shirt.
Colour matching balloon and T-shirt the same colour.

Where Is My Dad?

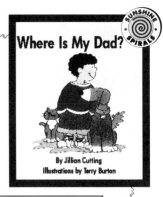

Where Is My Dad?
By Jillian Cutting
Illustrations by Terry Burton

<table>
<tr><td>Teaching Points for Set 1 Book 8:</td><td>sight words - a he in is it no the
letter recognition - d h i n
focus - questions - yes no
mum dad</td></tr>
</table>

Where Is My Dad?

Introducing the story

Before reading the story ask the children:

Where do you live? Is it in a house/flat/bungalow?

What room do you sleep in?

What room or rooms have a television in them?

What room do you cook in?

What room do you wash in?

The Oral Story-telling

Tim lived on a farm in the country. One day he wanted to ask his dad a question but he couldn't see him anywhere.

"Perhaps he is on the tractor?" thought Tim. Tim looked but his dad wasn't there.

"Perhaps he is in the barn?" thought Tim, but his dad wasn't there.

"Perhaps he is in the hen house?" thought Tim, but his dad wasn't there.

"Perhaps he is in the kitchen?" thought Tim but his dad wasn't there either.

"Perhaps he is in the bedroom?" thought Tim but his dad wasn't there.

There was one room Tim hadn't visited. Do you know which one it was? Just then Tim heard the T.V. "I bet my dad is watching T.V." said Tim and he ran downstairs. He saw Dad sitting in the chair in front of the T.V.

"Don't watch T.V. Come and play with me," said Tim. But his dad didn't answer. Tim went closer and he saw that Dad was fast asleep. "Wake up Dad!" said Tim and he switched off the T.V.

Reading the Text

See Introduction: Reading the Text, p.8.

Talking about the Story

Ask the children:

Can you remember all the places where Tim looked for his dad?

Where was Dad all the time?

Why do you think that Dad was asleep?

What do you think happened after Tim's dad woke up?

Follow-up Activities

• Game: "Hunt the thimble."

Make two flash cards, one with 'Yes' and one with 'No' written on them.

Hide a small object somewhere in the classroom.

Let the children ask questions to try to find out where you have hidden it.

Hold up the appropriate flash card as the answer to their questions, e.g. "Is it on the table?" Teacher holds up the 'No' card.

Is it on the desk? Teacher holds up 'Yes' card.

Is it under a book on the desk? Teacher holds up 'Yes' card and tells the child to go and look under the book.

When the children are used to this let them 'hide' the object and be the teacher with the cards for the others in the group.

• Give each child a copy of the photocopy master 8. Ask the children to circle the objects which have been hidden in the kitchen. There are pictures at the top to help them.

• Make a word.

This can be played either by using the blackboard or by writing the words on to a piece of paper.

The teacher writes 'in' on the board and three other letters as shown below. The children take it in turns to make up new words using the letters. This can be extended to building new words from other simple letter combinations, e.g. 'and' 'at' 'id'.

p			h			d		
d	—	in	s	—	at	k	—	id
w			f			h		

Mum's Hat

Introducing the Story

This is a story about a mum who lost her hat. She looked all over the house.

Where do you think she looked?

Have you ever lost anything and had to look all over your house for it?

Where did you find it?

Reading the Text

See Introduction: Reading the Text, p.8.

Follow-up Activities

• Game: "Guess what room I am in?"

Teachers gives clues, e.g.

I am in a room with taps. Where am I?
In this room I brush my teeth. Where am I?
In this room I have a bath. Where am I?

I am in a room where I like to sit. Where am I?
In this room there is a T.V. Where am I?
In this room there is a sofa. Where am I?

I am in a room with curtains. Where am I?
In this room there is a cupboard. Where am I?

In this room there is a bed. Where am I?

• Sing the song.

My hat has three corners. (Hand action. Point at head.)
Three corners has my hat. (Draw a triangle in the air.)
And if it didn't have three corners (Draw triangle in the air.)
It wouldn't be my hat. (Point at head.)

Verse 2.   This is sung as before but this time omit the word 'hat' wherever it occurs.

Verse 3.   This is sung as above but omit 'corners' and 'hat'.

Verse 4.   This is sung as above but omit 'corners' 'hat' and 'three'.

• Adults and their young.

Talk with the children about the different names for adults and their young.

cats and kittens; dogs and puppies; ducks and ducklings; horses and foals; cows and calves; sheep and lambs; bears and cubs.

When the children are familiar with these they could divide into teams and one team could ask the other the names of either the adults to the young or vice versa.

Letter shapes

D   d

H   h

I   i

N   n

Dad's Present

Introducing the Story

The aim of this story is to consolidate the sight vocabulary that the children have met in the previous stories. Before looking at the text ask the children what they think could be in Dad's parcel. Explain the convention of the 'thought bubbles' (which is also used in Set 1 Book 7) and check that the child can identify each object.

Reading the Text

Read the text on p.18 to the child.

Encourage the child to read the text on p.19 to you. Let the child lead the reading as far as possible. Encourage the child to take home the book and read the stories to the adult.

Follow-up Activities

• Consolidation of the core vocabulary through writing.

Make a 'Yes' and 'No' book.

Fold a sheet of A3 into eight sections and split along the seams so that it makes eight pages.

Staple down the spine.

Cut cards such as old Birthday or Christmas cards into seven squares approximately 6cms x 6cms.

Leave the cover page blank and on to each of the remaining right hand pages sellotape one of these squares down the left hand side so that the card makes a flap.

Draw round each of the squares made by the flap with a pencil so that the child can see clearly the area within which she or he may draw.

Draw a small box in the bottom right hand corner of this square big enough for the child to write 'Yes' or 'No' in the box.

Using a highlighter pen write the sentence, 'Is Mum (or Dad) in here?' under each card. The child goes over the words with a pencil and then may draw the answer on the page that he or she wishes. Children who can manage to write without the highlighter support should be encouraged to do so. e.g. The child may draw a rabbit under the first card and write 'No' in the box.

Then the child may draw a picture of a cat under the next, etc. On one page the child draws either Mum or Dad and writes 'Yes'.

The child asks his or her teacher or peers to guess whether Mum or Dad is under the card by reading the question each time and then showing the answer.

Note: This is a very simple book to make and children have many happy hours asking adults to guess and are very happy when they get it wrong.

• Game: "Guess the parcel."

Wrap up some objects and play like pass the parcel. The group passes round the parcel and at a given point they stop and the child holding the parcel has to feel it and guess its contents.

• Read to the children the poem "Cats" by Eleanor Farjeon (Young Puffin Book of Verse).

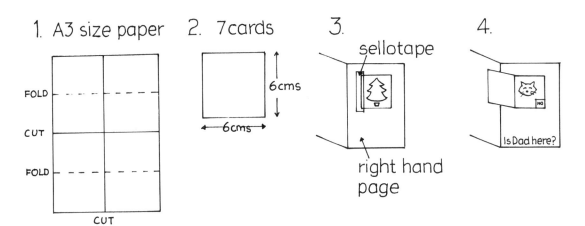

1. A3 size paper 2. 7 cards 3. 4.

FOLD CUT FOLD CUT

6cms 6cms

sellotape

right hand page

Is Dad here?

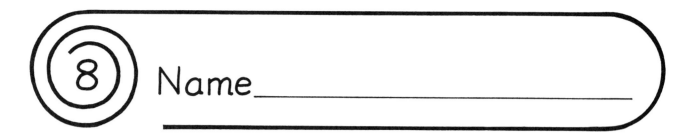

Where are they?

Put a circle around each of the hidden objects.

The Dragon

Teaching Points for Set 1 Book 9:

sight words - big in is it the
letter recognition - g s u v
focus - story book language
         e.g. dragon castle giant

The Dragon

Introducing the Story

Before reading the story ask the children:

What do you think a dragon looks like?

What do you think a dragon eats?

Where do you think a dragon lives?

Have you ever seen a dragon?

The Oral Story-Telling

I'm going to tell you about my friend Sam who lives in the house next door to mine. There is a dragon living in his house. He knows it is there but he never sees it. Sometimes it hides in the bathroom. He can see its shadow on the mirror. Sometimes it hides in the bedroom and he sees its shadow on the wall. Sometimes it hides in the kitchen.

When he went for a ride in the family car he found out that it hides in the garage. When he looked out of the window he saw that it sometimes hides in the garden.

What do you think Sam saw on the ground that showed him that the dragon was close by?

Showing the Story

Before looking at the text share the pictures with the children. See if they can spot the dragon on each page. Encourage the children to identify the places where the dragon hides - in the house, in the bathroom, in the bedroom, in the kitchen, in the garage, in the garden. Ensure that the vocabulary of 'hides' is part of your

introduction, e.g. "The dragon in this story hides in different places. Can you see where he hides?"

Reading the Text

See Introduction: Reading the Text, p.8.

Talking about the Story

Some questions to ask:

Do you think the little boy knew the dragon was there?

Do you think he is a friendly dragon?

How big do you think the dragon is?

Look at page eight. What do you think will happen next?

Follow-up Activities

• Match and colour. Photocopy the photocopy master 9 (Activity Book A5).

The child has to match the silhouette to the picture, and then he or she may colour the picture.

• Say the poem and encourage the children to join in with the repeated verses:

I thought I saw a dragon
Sitting on a stair
I quickly looked behind me
But he wasn't there.

I thought I saw a dragon
Sitting on a chair
I quickly looked behind me
But he wasn't there.

I thought I saw a dragon
Sitting in his lair
I quickly looked behind me
But he wasn't there.

I know I saw a dragon
Where ever can he be?
I know I saw a dragon
HELP he's after me!

- Read the story to the whole class, "There's no such thing as a dragon" by Jack Kent (Picture Puffin).

The Big Big Mountain

Introducing the Story

Before reading the story ask the children:

Have you ever visited a castle?

Who lives in a castle?

Have you ever built a sand castle?

What happens to a sand castle?

Showing the Story

Before looking at the text with the children show them the pictures and tell them the story.

Encourage them to join in with the refrain as they become familiar with it.

Then let them point and voice match the text as they say it with you.

Finally re-tell the story to the children leaving gaps for them to supply the missing words.

Reading the Text

As the children will now be very familiar with the story encourage them to point and voice match as they read.

Follow-up Activities

- Encourage the children to become confident with writing the sight words 'a big'.

  Give each child a sheet of A4 paper and draw four boxes as large as possible down the right hand side.

  Ask the children to draw a mountain, a castle, a giant and a table in the boxes.

  Write on the board or on to separate pieces of card the words 'a big big ...'

  The children look at these words and then try to write 'a big, big', without copying, leading up to each drawing.

- Song: "It's raining, it's pouring."

  It's raining, It's pouring.
  The old man is snoring.
  He hit his head on the bottom of the bed
  And couldn't get up in the morning.

- Read the children the story, "Funnybones" by Janet and Allan Ahlberg (Picture Lions).

- Read the children the story, "A Dark, Dark Tale" by Ruth Brown (Hippo).

Letter shapes

G g
S s
U u
V v

Who Is In The Lift?

Introducing the Story

Look at the pictures with the children and talk about the convention of thought bubbles. Prepare the noun vocabulary orally by reading the text to the children.

The aim of this book is to consolidate the sight words introduced in the earlier stories. Let the child share reading the text to you but as far as possible let the child lead the reading.

Follow-up Activities

• See the writing activity on p.41.

Make a similar book with flaps that hides the answers.

Let the children cut out objects from an old catalogue to stick behind the flaps.

Write the word for these objects on to card for each child. The child writes the sentence 'Is it a ...', endeavouring to write these sight words without copying. He or she uses the object card for the final noun. Sometimes the hidden object should match with the text and sometimes it should not. The child can then ask any interested adult or peer what they think will be below the flap. The greatest joy comes when the person gets it wrong!

• Guess the rhyming riddle?

I wondered what was in the lift
Something that rhymes with mat.
This animal has nice soft fur
In the lift was a ....

I wondered what was in the lift
Something that rhymes with log.
This is an animal that sometimes barks
In the lift was a ....

I wondered what was in the lift
Something that rhymes with house.
This animal is small and has a long tail
In the lift was a ....

I wondered what was in the lift
Something that rhymes with chair.
This animal is big and growls
In the lift was a ....

I wondered what was in the lift
Something that rhymes with heard.
This creature has wings to fly
In the lift was a ....

I wondered what was in the lift
Something that rhymes with box.
This animal has a bushy tail
In the lift was a ....

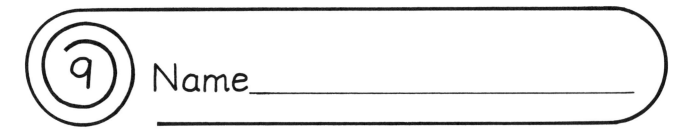

9 Name_____

Match and colour

Draw a line from the silhouettes to the pictures, then colour the picture.

Who Ate the Bananas?

Who Ate
the Bananas?

By Jillian Cutting
Illustrations by Jan van der Voo

Teaching Points for Set 1 Book 10:

sight words - help me not said
will you
letter recognition - d f j k l
focus - speech marks

Who Ate the Bananas?

Introducing the Story

Before reading the story ask the children:

What do you think elephants like to eat?

What do you think snakes like to eat?

What do you think tigers like to eat?

What do you think parrots like to eat?

What do you think monkeys like to eat?

What do you like to eat?

The Oral Story-Telling

One day the animals went for a walk. It was nearly teatime and they were very hungry. "I know a banana tree which has delicious ripe bananas on it. Let's go there and eat them for our tea," said Elephant. But what do you think they found? All the bananas had been eaten and all that was left was their skins! They all asked, "Who ate the bananas?"

"Not me," said the elephant.
"Not me," said the snake.
"Not me," said the tiger.
"Not me," said the parrot.
"Not me," said the monkey.

Just then they heard a crunching noise and a munching noise. They went down the path and there sitting on the grass was a little boy eating the last banana!

Reading the Text

See Introduction: Reading the Text, p.8.

Talking about the Story

Some questions to ask:

Do you like bananas?

Can you eat the skins?

Can you think of any other fruit where we don't eat the skin?

Can you think of any fruit where you do eat the skin?

Follow-up Activities

• Make a banana sandwich.

Share it with the group.

Talk about how bananas grow in bunches. Look at the title page to see a tree and how the bananas grow on it.

• Say the rhyme using the names of the children in the group.

Five ripe bananas in a bowl by the door
(Child's name) *came and ate one and then there were four.*

Four ripe bananas growing on a tree
.... came and ate one and then there were three.

Three ripe bananas looking good to chew
.... came and ate one and then there were two.

Two ripe bananas sitting in the sun
.... came and ate one and then there was one.

One last banana, there for all to see
Who came and ate it. ME!

• Spot the changes. Give each child a copy of the photocopy master 10 (Activity Book A6) and ask the child to see what is different in the picture below. Can they put a circle around ten things that are different? (parrot's beak, elephant's tail, elephant's tusks, monkey's tail, flower petals, snake pattern, apple on tree, bananas, butterfly markings, banana skin)

Help Me!

Introducing the Story

Before reading the text ask the children:

What do you do to help in your home?

What can you do to help me in the classroom?

Reading the Text

See Introduction: Reading the Text, p.8.

Follow-up Activities

• Ask the children if they know who can help them in the following situations:

If you want to cross a road?

If you fall over?

If you have a toothache?

If you feel sick?

If you get lost?

If there is a fire?

• Sing the song, "Help me wind my ball of wool" from "This Little Puffin".

Help me wind my ball of wool.
Hold it gently do not pull.
Wind the wool and wind the wool,
A-round A-round A-round.

• Read the class the story, "The Enormous Turnip" (Ladybird).

• The reading/writing connection.

Write out for each child the sentence "I will help you," across the top of a piece of paper.

The child then names four helpers, e.g. policeman, dentist, teacher, caretaker.

The teacher writes 'said the policeman', 'dentist' and so on down the right hand side of the child's paper.

The child looks at the sentence "I will help you," and then folds back this sentence and tries to write it from memory. At the first attempt he or she is likely to need to look again but the child should aim to be able to do it without looking by the last sentence.

> " I will help you,"
> _ _ _ _ _ _ _ _ _ _ _ _ _ _
> (fold back here)
>
> "   ," said the policeman.
>
> "   ," said the dentist.
>
> "   ," said the teacher.
>
> "   ," said the caretaker.

Cleaning the Car

Introducing the Story

Ask the children to look at the title page and then answer the questions:

What do you think Dad is going to do?

Will he wash the car on his own?

Who do you think will help him?

Reading the Text

Encourage the children to read the words they have already met in the other stories. They might need help with the words 'my sister', 'my brother', and the sentence, "Who will come for a drive?"

Follow-up Activities

• Ask the children:

Does this story remind you of any other story you know?

Why didn't the family want to help Dad?

Should Dad let them have a drive in the car?

• Draw attention to the speech marks.

Read the story again.

Let the child read the words within the speech marks, while you read the remaining text.

• Letter recognition: 'd', 'f', 'j', 'k', 'l'.

Write all the letter shapes on the board and talk about forming the letters as you do so. The children make the initial sound of the letter as it is written.

Name an object and the children say what letter it starts with.

Give a letter sound and this time the children have to offer words that start with the letter sound.

• Sing the following song to the tune of "Here we go round the Mulberry Bush"

This is the way we clean the car,
Clean the car, clean the car.
This is the way we clean the car
On a sunny Sunday morning.

This is the way we hose down the car.
This is the way we sponge off the dirt.
This is the way we wash the windows.
This is the way we polish the car.
Now the car is nice and clean.

• Say the following rhyme fitting in different children's names and choosing different jobs to be done around the classroom, some nicer than others, e.g. pick up the books; tidy the library; ring the bell; collect the pencils; tidy the Lego; sing a song; turn on the T.V.; get out the paints.
Who will help me .....? (choose a job)
Who will it be?
..... (child's name) help me .....

Child answers: No, not me! or Yes, please, me!

• Read to the children "The Little Red Hen" (Ladybird). Also share with them "The Little Yellow Chick", Sunshine Books (Heinemann) which comes in both standard format and big book version.

Letter shapes

D   d

F   f

J   j

K   k

L   l

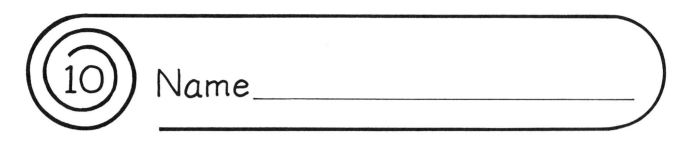

Spot ten changes

Put a circle round the change in the second picture.

Night

Teaching Points for Set 2 Book 1:	sight words - away on went letter recognition: d o u w focus - night-time/daytime

Night

Introducing the Story

Before reading the story ask the children:

   When do you go to bed?

   Is it dark outside or light outside when you go to bed?

   In the winter is it dark or light when you go to bed?

   What animals are awake at night and sleep in the day? (owl, hedgehog, mouse)

   What might you see in the sky at night?

   What might you see in the sky during the day?

The Oral Story-Telling

Once upon a time there was a little tree. It stood all alone in the middle of a field. But was the tree lonely? No, because each night some night-time friends came to visit the little tree. An owl would come and sit on a high branch. A squeaky mouse and a snuffly hedgehog came to sit by the trunk. Up in the sky the moon shone down on the night-time friends. Time passed and the moon went away.

"It is nearly morning," said the wise old owl. "It is time for me to go to bed."

"And for us too," said the hedgehog and the mouse. So they all went away.

Was the tree lonely? No, because each day some daytime friends came to visit the little tree. Can you guess who they were?

Reading the Text

See Introduction: Reading the Text, p.8.

Talking about the Story

Some questions to ask:

   Can you remember the animals that came to visit the little tree?

   Why do you think they left in the morning?

   Can you remember the animals that visited the tree in the day?

   What do you think they will do when the night-time comes?

Follow-up Activities

• On a copy of the photocopy master 11 (Activity Book A7) put a ring round the ten hidden animals (badger, squirrel, cat, rabbit, owl, mouse, hedgehog, bird, butterfly, fox).

• A Night-time song.

When all the cows were sleeping,
And the sun had gone to bed,
Up jumped the scarecrow
And this is what he said.

"I'm a dingle, dangle scarecrow
With a flippy floppy hat.
I can shake my hands like this
And shake my feet like that."

When all the hens were roosting
And the moon behind a cloud,
Up jumped the scarecrow
And shouted very loud.

"I'm a dingle dangle scarecrow," etc.

• Say the round:

Morning is come.
Night time away,
Rise with the sun
and welcome the day.

• Game: "Day and night-time".

Make two cards for each player.

Write 'day' on one and 'night' on the other.

The teacher then makes statements and the children have to decide whether this would take place in the daytime or the night time, e.g.

The stars are shining very brightly.

I can see my shadow.

We have a picnic by the sea.

• Read "Good Night Owl" by Pat Hutchins (Picture Puffin).

Go!

Introducing the Story

Before reading the story ask the children:

Have you ever watched racing cars on the T.V?

What do racing cars look like?

How fast do racing cars go?

Showing the Story

Let the children tell you the colours of all the different cars. Talk about why the man has to start the race with a flag. (It is because of the noise.) Ask the children to guess which car they think will win the race. What happened to the green car?

Reading the Text

See Introduction: Reading the Text, p.8.

Follow-up Activities

• Listen to the starting letter.

Write on the blackboard the letters 'w' and 'd'.

Say a word that starts with either letter. Ask a child to come up and write the starting letter of the word under the letters on the board. e.g. wet, went, water, window, wood, dog, daisy, duck, did, do.

• Sing the song: "Five little racing cars".

Five little racing cars
Standing in a row.
The starter waved his flag
And they began to go.
The red car went ....zooom.

Repeat the first three lines each time.

The blue car went....zooom
The yellow car went....zooom
The black car went....zooom
The green car went.....SSSSS.

• Make a flag to start a race.

You will need:

A piece of material or a piece of paper.
A piece of dowling or a stick.

Cut the material or paper into a rectangle. Ask the children to help you decorate it. Fix it to the piece of dowling or stick.

• Have a race.

Using 'Post-it' notes with a dot of colour, label the children the following colours: red; blue; yellow; black; green.

Have races either in the hall or outside. The race starts when the flag is lowered but as you lower the flag call out one of the colours and only the children with that colour should run to the finish line.

Going to Grandma's

Introducing the Story

The aim of this story is to consolidate the sight vocabulary that the children have met in the previous stories. Before reading the text ask the children to identify the various vehicles. See if they can find the words plane, train, bus, jeep, cart, and horse on the pages.

Reading the Text

Let the child share the reading with you but as far as possible, let the child lead the reading. Encourage the child to take the book home and read it to an adult.

Follow up Activities

• What do you call your grandparents?

Ask the children what they call their grandparents. Write the different suggestions on the board, e.g. Gran, Granny, Grandma, Nanny. Ask the children to put up their hands when the one they use is suggested. Make a bar chart of the results. Some children might like to ask other teachers what they call their grandparents.

• Make a vehicle collage.

Let the children collect pictures from magazines and newspapers. Let them cut them out and arrange them on a large sheet of paper. This could be of a mixture of vehicles or separate sheets for the different ones, e.g. cars, lorries, bicycles.

• Look at a map of the world.

Ask the children, "Where does Grandma, or Grandad, live?" Bring in postcards from places where Grandparents or other relatives live.

Letter shapes

D   d

O   o

U   u

W   w

11

Name_____

Find ten animals

Put a ring around all the hidden animals.

Elephant Walk

Elephant Walk

By Joy Cowley
Illustrations by Gary Rees

Teaching Points for Set 2 Book 2:

sight words - down into the went
letter recognition - d k l y
focus - rhyme recognition

Elephant Walk

Introducing the Story

Before reading the story ask the children :

What animals are too big or too dangerous to be pets?

Where could you see these animals in this country?

Have you ever been to the zoo?

Which big animal is your favourite?

What might happen if an elephant came to school?

The Oral Story-Telling

Nellie the elephant wanted an adventure. She decided to go for a walk to see what she could find. She walked down the High Street. "What's this place full of toys?" Nellie wondered. She saw a board on wheels. "This looks fun for a ride," said Nellie and she stood on it. What shop do you think Nellie was in?

Nellie went into the shop next door. "What's this place full of bats, balls, skis and rackets?" wondered Nellie. She took them all off the shelves and put them on the floor. What shop do you think Nellie was in?

Then Nellie went into the shop next door. "What's this place with lots of clothes and dresses?" wondered Nellie. And she put one dress on her head. What shop do you think Nellie was in?

Then Nellie went into the shop next door. "What's this place full of books to buy?" wondered Nellie and she started to read a book about elephants. What shop do you think Nellie was in?

Then Nellie went into a big building. There were children sitting on the floor and a teacher showing them a nice big book. "What's this place that looks such fun?" wondered Nellie. Where do you think Nellie was?

The children all jumped up. "Hello, Nellie," they said. "It's time you went back home." So they took Nellie back to the zoo. "What an adventure," said Nellie. "I wonder where I'll go tomorrow!"

Reading the Story

See Introduction: Reading the Text, p.8.

Talking about the Story

Some questions to ask:

Can you remember where Nellie went on her adventure? (toy shop, sports shop, dress shop, book shop, school)

Where do you think Nellie will go tomorrow?

Follow-up Activities

• Song: "Nellie the Elephant packed her trunk."

Nellie the Elephant packed her trunk
And said goodbye to the circus
Off she went with a trumpety trump
Trump, trump, trump.
The head of the herd was calling
Far, far away
They met one night, in the pale moonlight
On the road to Mandalay.

- Elephant jokes

  How can you tell if an elephant's been in your fridge?
  You can see its footprints in the butter.

  What's grey and red all over?
  An embarrassed elephant.

  Why couldn't the two elephants go swimming?
  Because they only had one pair of trunks between them.

  Why did the elephant go to the dentist?
  It had a terrible tuskache!

- Ask the children to practise writing the sight words on the photocopy master 12 (Activity Book A8). When they have finished they should number the pictures in the correct sequence.

- Read the children "The Elephant and the Bad Baby" by Elfrida Vipont (Hamish Hamilton).

- Read "Elmer the Elephant" by David McKee (Beaver).

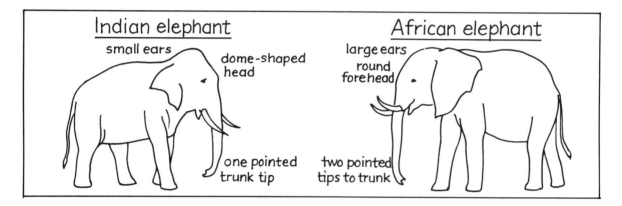

Cactus Town

Introducing the Story

Before reading the story ask the children:

  What is a cactus?

  Where might you find them?

  Would you like to climb one?

Talk to the children about what a rodeo is and what sort of stunts happen, e.g. riding a bucking bronco; riding a bull; rope tricks with a lasso.

Reading the Text

See Introduction: Reading the Text, p.8.

Talking about the Story

Some questions to ask:

  Can you remember all the different ways people travelled to the rodeo? (bus, train, truck, car, horse)

  Which way would you have liked to travel?

  Would you like to ride a bucking bronco?

Follow-up Activities

- Find the rhyming partner.

  Make approximately twelve cards of six rhyming pairs, e.g. down/town; went/sent; truck/luck; king/sing; train/rain; cars/stars.

  Select sufficient pairs of rhyming words for the number of players. Give each child a card and check that he or she can read it. Quietly prompt any player who needs help. Then each player finds their rhyming partner and the partners say their rhyming words. When all the partners have been found deal out the cards again for players to find their new partners.

- Letter tracking.

  Give each child a sheet of print from either a newspaper or a magazine, and a crayon. Give each child a letter to search for - d, k, l or y. Every time the children find a letter they mark it. After a few minutes stop the children and ask them how many they have found. Children could then swap letters and search again.

The Diver

Introducing the Story

Before reading the story talk to the children about the equipment that divers use:

Why do they wear a wet suit?

What are goggles for? Snorkel? Flippers?

Look at p.17. Why do you think there is a cross on the map?

Reading the Text

Let the child lead the reading as far as possible but support the child with new vocabulary, e.g. 'put', 'my'.

Follow-up Activities

• Game: "Treasure search".

Draw a grid (6 squares by 6 squares) on the blackboard. Write the numbers down the columns and colours across the top (red, green, blue, yellow, white, black). The teacher selects the square where the treasure is 'hidden' and writes the reference on a piece of paper, (e.g. white, 4). The children take it in turn to select a grid reference   (e.g. blue,2) and shows the group which square they have selected. If the treasure is not found at that reference the square is crossed off and another child chooses a reference. When the treasure has been discovered the child can select the next hiding place.

• A sea song.

Teach the children the song :

A sailor went to sea, sea, sea,
To see what he could see,see, see,
But all that he could see, see, see
Was the bottom of the deep blue sea, sea, sea.

Letter shapes

D   d

K   k

L   l

Y   y

	red	green	blue	yellow	white	black
1		X				
2	X					X
3			X			
4				X	🗝	
5		X		X		
6						

12

Name_____

_____

Where did the elephant go?

The 🐘 went into

the [ ]

The _____ _____

[ ]

The _____ _____

_____ [ ]

The _____ _____

_____ [ ]

The _____ _____

_____ [ ]

Go over the dots, then write the words on the next lines. Put a number in the box to show where the elephant went 1st, 2nd, 3rd, 4th and 5th.

At the Zoo

At the Zoo

By Jill Eggleton
Illustrations by Celia Canning

Teaching Points for Set 2 Book 3:	**sight words** - had he his in **letter recognition** - h s t **focus** - full stop

At the Zoo

Introducing the Story

Before reading the story ask the children:

   What animals would you see in a zoo?

   Which animal do you think is the tallest?

   Which animal has very big ears?

   Which big animal likes to roll in the mud?

   Which animal can look like a log in the water?

   Which long-tailed animal can swing through the trees?

   Who looks after all the animals?

The Oral Story-Telling

John, the zookeeper was very busy. All the animals were sick. Can you guess what was wrong with the giraffe? It had a sore neck. Can you guess what was wrong with the Hippo? It had a sore stomach. Can you guess what was wrong with the tiger? It had a sore leg. Can you guess what was wrong with the elephant? It had a sore ear. Can you guess what was wrong with the crocodile? It had a sore tooth. Can you guess what was wrong with the monkey? It had a sore tail. John worked hard all day helping the animals to get better. Then he went home and sat in the chair. Guess what? John had a sore head!

Reading the Text

See Introduction: Reading the Text, p.8.

Talking about the Story

Ask the children:

Can you remember what was wrong with the hippo, tiger, elephant, crocodile, monkey and Jack?

Follow-up Activities

• Sing the Song: "Daddy's going to take us to the zoo tomorrow."

• Guess the riddle.

   I have long legs.
   I like eating leaves.
   I have a long neck.
   I am a .....

   I have a big mouth.
   I like water.
   I like to roll in mud.
   I am a .....

   I am very big.
   People say I can remember things.
   I have a long nose.
   I am a .....

   I am very fierce.
   I eat raw meat.
   I have a striped coat.
   I am a .....

   I swim in the water.
   I have sharp teeth.
   I have a rough and scaly skin.
   I am a .....

   I have a long tail.
   I swing through the trees.
   I like bananas.
   I am a .....

Grandad's Ride

Introducing the Story

Before reading the story ask the children:

What sort of things can you have a ride on?

Do you think your Grandad would go on any of these?

Look at the pictures in this story. What is Grandad riding on?

Reading the Text

See Introduction: Reading the Text, p.8.

In this story the children should be able to lead the reading of "He had a..." as they have met this vocabulary before.

Talking about the Story

Which ride do you think Grandad enjoyed the most?

Which ride do you think was the fastest?

Which ride do you think was the slowest?

Have you ever seen people in a balloon?

Follow-up Activities

• Make a bar chart about transport.

Divide the categories according to the number of wheels, e.g. one wheel, two wheels, three wheels, four wheels, more than four wheels.

Ask the children to collect pictures of things with wheels. Let them cut them out and stick them into the correct column. After a period of time see which vehicle has the most pictures.

• Sing the song:

Grandpa went for a ride one day
Over the hills and far away
What do you think he chose to ride?
His shiny new red bike.
(Children pedal with hands)

Repeat the first three lines each time.

Add the new line and actions:

His roaring motor bike
(Children make revving motion with hands.)

His speedy motor car
(Children hold steering wheel.)

His beautiful coloured balloon
(Make shape of balloon with hands above heads and sway gently.).

TRANSPORT				
One wheel	Two wheels	Three wheels	Four wheels	More than four wheels

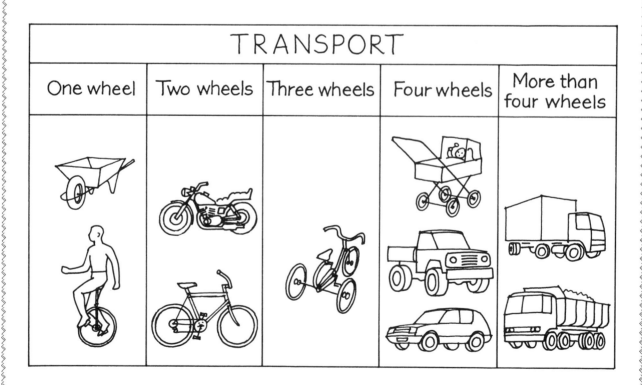

Where Is the Money?

Introducing the Story

Before reading the story ask the children:

What do you like to buy at the shops?

What things do you put in your pocket?

What does your mum or dad say about full pockets?

Reading the Text

With a partner let the children practise reading this story.

The aim of this book is to consolidate the sight vocabulary the children have already met in the previous stories. Ask the children to read the story to you in pairs.

Encourage the children to take this book home and read it to an adult.

Follow-up Activities

• What's missing?

Collect about ten objects and place them on a tray. If possible replicate those from the story i.e. snail, feather, string, whistle, shell, money.

Cover the objects with a cloth and remove one. Take the cloth away. Ask the children to tell you what you have removed. It is possible to play this by removing an additional object each time.

When the tray is empty see if the children can recall all the objects and as they do so replace them on the tray.

• Shopping.

Tell the children they are to be customers in a shop and give each of them five counters. You are the shop keeper and you are going to try to sell them different things **but** they only want to buy things that start with the sounds 'h' or 't' or 's'.

Offer each child three things to buy and let them choose, e.g. "James, would you like to buy a dog, a jumper or a hat?"

If he selects correctly remove one counter. The winner is the first child to have no counters left.

• Letter recognition.

Give each child a copy of the photocopy master 13 (Activity Book A9). Before they write on the page ask the children to 'draw' the letters 'h' 't'and 's'in the air. Check that each child is forming these letters correctly. Ask each child what each letter is called and what sound it makes.

Letter shapes

H h

S s

T t

What is the first letter?

h   t   s

Choose the correct first letter and write it in the box.

Dinnertime

Dinnertime
By Joy Cowley
Illustrations by Tracey Moroney

Teaching Points for Set 2 Book 4:

sight words - some want
letter recognition - b g o
focus - food vocabulary

Dinnertime

Introducing the Story

Before reading the story ask the children :

What is your favourite food?

Do you always eat everything you are given?

What food do you not like?

The Oral Story-Telling

One day Dad was looking after the baby. He was making her some lunch. "Do you want some meat?" asked Dad. "No!" said the baby. "Do you want some rice?" asked Dad. "No!" said the baby. "Do you want some cheese?" asked Dad. "No!" said the baby. "Do you want some bread?" asked Dad. "No!" said the baby. "Do you want some milk?" asked Dad. "No!" said the baby.

Dad did not know what to do. He didn't want to waste all the food. Then he remembered Ginger, the cat. "Here puss, puss," he called. "Come and eat this food." And he put all the food on the floor for Ginger.

What do you think the baby said? She said, "No,no, I **want** my dinner!"

Reading the Text

See Introduction: Reading the Text, p.8.

Talking about the Story

Ask the children :

Can you remember what Dad gave the baby?

What did Dad decide to do with all the food?

What did the baby do when she saw the cat?

Follow-up Activities

• Game: "What's the time Mr.Wolf?"

This game is best played in the hall or in an open space. The teacher stands facing the group of children. They are at one end of the room and she or he is at the other. The children step cautiously forward asking in unison "What's the time Mr Wolf?" Mr Wolf (i.e. the teacher) answers: one o'clock, two o'clock, three o'clock etc. The children step forward a little and ask the question again. At some point the wolf will answer "Dinnertime" and run to catch any children within reach. Now another child can be the 'wolf' and the game starts again. If a child touches the wolf before she or he turns around, that child becomes the wolf.

• Clap the rhyme: "Pease porridge hot".

Pease porridge hot,
Pease porridge cold,
Pease porridge in the pot
Nine days old.
Some like it hot,
Some like it cold,
Some like it in the pot,
Nine days old.

Children stand opposite a partner. At the word 'Pease' each partner claps their own sides. At the word 'porridge' each partner claps their own hands together. At the word 'hot' the partners clap their hands together . The clapping pattern is repeated for the next words 'Pease, porridge cold'. For the line 'Pease porridge in the pot' the partners clap their own sides on the word 'pease' and their own hands together for 'porridge'. At the words 'in the' partners clap their right hands together, and at the word 'pot' they clap left hands together.

The clapping pattern continues for the rest of the verse.

- Read the story "What's the time Mr Wolf?" by Colin Hawkins (Picture Lions).
- With a partner children can compose a menu of their favourite meal. The teacher could write a model menu on the board to help children organize their writing under the correct headings.

Menu

Starter:	Tomato soup or Fish cake
Main Course:	Sausages or Burgers
Vegetables:	Potatoes Peas
Pudding:	Ice cream or Chocolate cake

The Grumposaur

Introducing the Story

Before reading the story ask the children :

Do you know the names of any dinosaurs? (Some names are given in Set 1 Book 1, but it would be useful to have a dinosaur book available to which children may refer.)

What do you think dinosaurs ate?

What size do you think they were?

Reading the Text

See Introduction: Reading the Text, p.8.

Talking about the Story

Some questions to ask:

What did the mother dinosaur offer her baby ? (food, drink, toys, friends, bed)

What did the baby dinosaur really want?

Why do you think he is called a Grumposaur?

Follow-up Activities

- What do you think these dinosaurs like to do:

Sleeposaurus; Songosaurus; Munchosaurus; Jumposaurus; Thumposaurus; Swimosaurus; Gigglosaurus?

- Read the children the story, "Longneck & Thunderfoot" by Helen Piers (Picture Puffin)
- Say the dinosaur poem :

I think I saw a dinosaur
Walking down the street.
I think I heard the pounding
And the thumping of his feet.

I think I saw a dinosaur
Walking near my school.
I think I heard him take a drink
And paddle in our pool.

I think I saw a dinosaur
He was as big as big could be.
I think I saw his beady eye
Looking down at me.

I thought I saw a dinosaur,
But my dad says that he fears
It can't have been a dinosaur.
They've been dead 80 million years.

- On the photocopy master 14 (Activity Book A10) practise writing the words, 'I want some'. Make sure the children start the letters at the right place.

Skiing

Introducing the Story

Before reading the story ask the children:

What is skiing?

Where do people ski?

When do people ski?

What do people wear when they ski?

Reading the Text

This story should be 'paired read' by the teacher and child. Expect the child to lead the reading of "I want a..." Help with the unfamiliar words.

Follow-up Activities

• Ask the children what you need to :

play football?

go swimming?

go horse riding?

do ballet dancing?

go ice skating?

• Make snowflake shapes from square pieces of white paper.

Fold a piece of paper about 20cms square in half and in half again so that it is a smaller square. Fold diagonally. Fold diagonally again. Cut patterned shapes at the edge of the folds. Unfold.

Stick the different shaped snowflakes on to a blue or black mount.

• Odd one out

Read the following descriptions to the children and ask them to identify the odd one out.

When I play football I take my football boots, my football shirt, my football socks and a cricket bat.

When I go swimming I take my swimming costume, a tennis ball and my towel.

When I go skating I take my bicycle, my ice skates and some warm clothes.

• Dress dolls in warm clothes and talk about clothes vocabulary.

Letter shapes

B b

G g

O o

Write the words

"I want some red 🍎🍎🍎,"
said the 🐴

"___ ___ ___ orange 🍊🍊🍊,"
said the 🐘

"___ ___ ___ yellow 🍐🍐🍐,"
said the 🐵

"___ ___ ___ green 🌸🌸🌸,"
said the 🐌

"___ ___ ___ black 🍇🍇🍇,"
said the 🐭

Write the missing words.

I Can Climb

I Can Climb

By Jill Eggleton
Illustrations by Philip Webb

Teaching Points for Set 2 Book 5:	sight words - can see we letter recognition - d e w focus - creature vocabulary

---

I Can Climb

Introducing the Story

Before reading the story ask the children:

Do you think a monkey could climb a tree?

Do you think a snake could climb a tree?

Do you think a leopard could climb a tree?

Do you think a spider could climb a tree?

Do you think an ant could climb a tree?

Do you think an elephant **should** climb a tree?

The Oral Story-Telling

Millie the monkey was always showing off. "I can do anything," she said. "I can swing with my tail from the branches. I can climb to the top of that tree." And off she climbed right to the top of the tree. Sammy the snake saw her "I can climb the tree," he said and up he went. Lennie the leopard saw Sammy the snake. "I can climb the tree," he said and up he went. Sally the spider saw Lennie up the tree. "I can climb the tree," she said and up she went. Annie the ant saw Sally the spider. "I can climb the tree," she said and up she went. Emma the elephant saw all the animals up the tree. "I can climb the tree," she said and she started to go up. But what do you think happened to the tree? It fell down!

Reading the Text

See Introduction: Reading the Text, p.8.

Talking about the Story

Ask the children if they can remember the animals that climbed the tree:

Which animal do you think could climb the tree quickly?

Which animal was the smallest to try to climb the tree?

Which animal would be the slowest to climb the tree?

Which animal should not try to climb trees?

Follow-up Activities

• Introducing adjectives

Ask the children to think about different animals that are light, heavy, tall, thin, wide, round. Encourage the children to try to describe the animals, e.g. as heavy as an elephant, as small as an ant, as long as a snake, as round as an owl.

Write down their suggestions on to a sheet of paper.

When you have collected all their ideas ask each child to try to draw one of the animals for you and paste it alongside the description.

• Ask the children to pretend they are animals. In pairs, or in a group they take it in turns to describe themselves and let the partner or group guess what they are. Encourage them to use adjectives like tall, small, heavy.

• Poem: "Walking through the jungle".

Encourage the children to join in the poem.

They could pretend to walk very carefully through the jungle and mime the actions of each animal.

Walking through the jungle
What did I see?
A baby monkey laughing
At me, me, me.

Walking through the jungle
What did I see?
A big lion roaring
At me, me, me.

Walking through the jungle
What did I see?
A slippery snake hissing
At me, me, me.

- Read the class a version of "The Enormous Turnip".

The Baby Turtle

Introducing the Story

Before reading the story ask the children:

Has anyone got a pet turtle?

Where do you think turtles like to live?

How big do you think turtles are?

Talk to the children about endangered animals and how turtles are now protected.

Collect some books or pictures of turtles and talk to the children about the differences between turtles and tortoises. (What do they eat? Where do they live?)

Reading the Text

See Introduction: Reading the Text, p.8.

Talking about the Story

Ask the children if they can describe the place where the baby turtle was born:

Was it somewhere hot or cold?

Do you think he liked it in the sand?

Do you think he liked meeting the crab?

Can you remember any other enemy of the baby turtle?

Where did the baby turtle like to be most of all?

Follow-up Activities

- Where do I come from?

Make a very simple book as described on p.41 (Set 1 Book 8).

Write the questions on the page and put the answers under the flap.

"Do I come from an egg?" said the bird. (Under the flap write the appropriate 'yes' or 'no'.)

"Do I come from an egg?" said the turtle.

"Do I come from an egg?" said the kitten.

"Do I come from an egg?" said the crocodile.

"Do I come from an egg?" said the puppy.

Let the children ask each other the questions and then raise the flap to see if their friend was right or wrong.

- Give each child a copy of the photocopy master 15 (Activity Book A11).

Encourage the children to write the words 'We can see' without copying.

- Rhyme: "Ten little turtles".

Ten little turtles
Standing in a line
Along came a sea-gull
And then there were nine.

Nine little turtles
Each had a mate
Along came a lobster
And then there were eight.

Eight little turtles
Hoped to go to heaven
Along came a shark
And then there were seven.

Seven little turtles
Were in quite a fix
Along came a crab
And then there were six.

Six little turtles
Went to have a dive
Along came an octopus
And then there were five.

Five little turtles
Went swimming one day
They knew that in the water
They were safe to play.

The Footprints

Introducing the Story

Before reading the story show the children the pictures and ask:

What might have made such enormous footprints?

Do you think the footprints belong to a person?

Do you think the footprints belong to an animal?

Reading the Text

This is an accumulative story which children often find easy to remember.

Check that the children can identify and label the different terrain that the monster has crossed.

Ask them to show you the words mud, sand, grass, snow, cave, and monster.

Let the children read the story to you in pairs and encourage them to use expression and intonation, building up to a climax!

Encourage them to take the book home and read it to an adult.

Follow-up Activities

- Use the text to perform an action walk towards the monster.

  Let the children say, "We can see footprints in the mud," and suggest that they walk slowly as though they had sticky mud on their shoes. "We can see footprints in the sand." Let them shuffle their feet as though moving through fine sand. "We can see footprints on the grass." Let them move the tall grass aside with their hands. "We can see footprints in the snow." The children could pretend to shiver and slide across the snow. "We can see footprints in the cave." Let them look nervous and glance from side to side. Finally you be the monster and chase them back through all the snow, grass, sand and mud until they get home.

- Make a hand print picture.

  Mix poster paint to a light consistency in several colours.

  Pour a little into a shallow dish.

  Let each child place their flat hand into the paint and then press it on to a sheet of paper.

If the hand prints overlap the effect is more interesting and can lead to colours changing, e.g. if blue and yellow are overlapped.

- Make a footprint picture.

  Use a thick felt tip pen and either draw around each child's foot or let the children draw around each other. Let the children cut out their footprint carefully. Each child can draw a line of glue along the toes of the footprint. These can then be stuck overlapping each other on to the outline shape of a monster or a bird, e.g. an owl. This is a very effective way of giving depth to a collage. The foot outline could be in black or a mixture of colours.

- Mime the story.

  This is a good story for a small group of children to mime to the class. Let one child be the monster hidden behind a piece of classroom furniture. The others in the group act out the journey. When they get near the 'cave' they look around and appear nervous. Finally they look behind the furniture and the 'monster' jumps out!

- Read to the class, "We're going on a bear hunt" by Michael Rosen (Walker).

Letter shapes

D d

E e

W w

15

Name_____
_____

What can we see?

We   can   see   a
We   can   see   a
We   can   see   a
___   ___   ___   __
___   ___   ___   __
___   ___   ___   __ monster

Draw the monster

Write the sentences. Then draw the monster.

A Journey

A Journey
By Jill Eggleton
Illustrations by Nick Price

Teaching Points for Set 2 Book 6:

sight words - are going
letter recognition - l m v z
focus - prediction

A Journey

Introducing the Story

Before reading the story ask the children:

What creatures might you meet on a jungle journey?

What creatures live in the trees?

What creatures live in the rivers?

The Oral Story-Telling

One day three friends set off on a journey. They wanted to explore the jungle. The smaller boy had been to the jungle before so he was able to tell his friends about everything on their journey.

He said, "We are going into the jungle. First we will be going over the mud, then we are going into the river."

The friends kept close together looking out for danger.

"I know," said the small boy, "We can go across the river walking on that log." The three friends walked on to the log.

"Just a minute," said the girl, "this log is moving."

"Oh no!" said one of the boys. They looked at the 'log' and saw that it had two beady eyes, a long snout and two rows of very sharp teeth.

"Help! Run!" said the small boy. What do you think the log really was?

Reading the Text

See Introduction: Reading the Text, p.8.

Talking about the Story

Ask the children:

Where did the friends go for their journey?

What gave them a surprise?

Do you think other creatures might be disguised as something else? What might a snake look like? A moth? A chameleon?

Look for a book on animal camouflage in the library.

Follow-up Activities

• Game: "Please Mr Crocodile".

The children line up on one side of the room and the teacher stands at the other side. The children chant together, "Please Mr Crocodile, may we cross your muddy river?" The teacher (crocodile) replies, "Not unless you've got the colour... (teacher chooses a colour)." All those children who are wearing something of that particular colour may cross. All others are out and line upon the crocodile's side. The game continues until there is no one asking to cross the river.

• Say the poem :

If you should meet a crocodile,
Don't take a stick and poke him;
Ignore the welcome in his smile,
Be careful not to stroke him.
For as he sleeps upon the Nile,
He thinner gets and thinner;
And whene'er you meet a crocodile
He's ready for his dinner.
(Anon)

• Read the children the story, "We're going on a Bear Hunt" by Michael Rosen (Walker Books).

Cat and Bird

Introducing the Story

Before reading the story ask the children :

Do you have a cat?

Does your cat like to chase birds in the garden?

Does your cat ever catch any birds?

Reading the Text

See Introduction: Reading the Text, p.8.

Talking about the Story

Look at the pictures together and ask the children, "What do you guess the cat might be thinking about on this page?" for each of pages 10-16.

Follow-up Activities

• Say the finger rhyme :

Five little pussy cats playing near the door;
One ran and hid inside and then there were four.
Four little pussy cats underneath a tree;
One heard a dog bark and then there were three.
Three little pussy cats thinking what to do;
One saw a little bird and then there were two.
Two little pussy cats sitting in the sun;
One ran to catch his tail and then there was one.
One little pussy cat looking for some fun;
He saw a butterfly and then there was none.

• Using the photocopy master 16 (Activity Book A12) ask the children to draw over the letter shapes (l, m, v, z) to make the picture. When the picture is complete, colour it in.

• Join in this little play.

You will need one child to be a worm; one child to be a bird; one child to be a cat; one child to be a dog and one child to be the dog's owner.

1st child (worm):

I am a little wriggly worm
Looking for my tea.
What's that noise that I can hear?
A bird is after me!

2nd child (bird):

I see a little wriggly worm.
I'd like it for my tea.
What's that noise that I can hear?
The cat is after me!

3rd child (cat):

I see a little hopping bird.
I'd like it for my tea.
What's that noise that I can hear?
The dog is after me!

4th child (dog):

I see a little furry cat.
I'd like it for my tea.
What's that noise that I can hear?
My owner's after me!

• Encourage birds to visit the school grounds.

Make a hanging feeder to attract birds. Mix bird seed, millet, chopped bacon rind, shelled peanuts and coconut. Add enough suet to make the mixture pliable. Thread a piece of string through the bottom of an empty yoghurt pot leaving some length by which to hang the feeder. Press the feed mixture into the pot and chill the mixture. Hang the pot by the string, within sight of the classroom, and this should attract garden birds, especially blue tits.

• Read to the children the story, "Rosie's Walk" by Pat Hutchins (Picture Puffin).

Letter shapes

L   l

M   m

V   v

Z   z

Where Are We Going, Grandad?

Introducing the Story

Before reading the story ask the children :

Where do you most like going on an outing? Do you like the seaside or the zoo?

In this story Grandad takes the children on rather a special trip. They are going to travel very fast indeed and be flying through the sky but they are not in an aeroplane. What could they be flying in and where are they going?

Reading the Text

This story repeats the vocabulary of the earlier stories in this book and the children should manage to read this text virtually unaided. The only unfamiliar word might be 'where' and it would be useful to draw children's attention to this word in the title.

Follow-up Activities

• Riddle time.

Ask the children the following riddles :

I am going somewhere where I shall see lots of animals.
I am going somewhere where I shall see lions, monkeys and penguins.
Where am I going?

I am going somewhere where I will need a special backpack for breathing.
I am going somewhere where I will travel by rocket.
Where am I going?

I am going somewhere where I need a special backpack for breathing.
I will see lots of fish where I am going.
Where am I going?

I am going somewhere where I will need my swimming costume.
I am going somewhere where there will be lots of sand.
Where am I going?

• Say the chant :

Grandad, grandad, where are we going?
Grandad, grandad, what are we going to do?
We are going to visit a jungle and see a crocodile.
That's what we're all going to do.

Grandad, grandad, where are we going?
Grandad, grandad, what are we going to do?
We are going to visit the moon in our special rocket.
That's what we're all going to do.

Grandad, grandad, where are we going?
Grandad, grandad, what are we going to do?
We going to have a rest now and close our eyes.
That's what we're all going to do.

• Ask the children to tell you about a special trip they have been on, such as a visit to a wildlife park, or to the seaside. They can bring in photographs to share with the class.

16

Name_____

Join the dots - l m v z

Draw over the letter shapes l m v and z to make the picture. Then colour.

The Space Monster

The Space Monster
By Jillian Cutting
Illustrations by Ian McCausland

Teaching Points for Set 2 Book 7:

sight words - going is to
letter recognition - qu r z
focus - space travel

The Space Monster

Introducing the Story

Before reading the story ask the children :

What can you see in the sky at night?

Do you think anyone lives on the moon?

What do you think a space monster would be like?

Have you seen any space programmes on the T.V?

The Oral Story-Telling

One day when I was very small my naughty brother told me a story. He thought I would be frightened but I wasn't. He told me about a bad space monster. "The space monster is coming," said my brother "The space monster is coming to Earth."

"I don't believe you," I said. "I have never seen a space monster."

"The spaceships went out and frightened it away," said my brother.

"The spaceships went Zap! Zap! Zap!"

"What happened to the space monster?" I asked.

"The space monster went away. It went away into the sun," said my brother, "but if you don't do what I say I will call it back again!"

"I don't believe you," I said "There is no such thing as a space monster."

I still don't believe him, do you?

Reading the Text

See Introduction: Reading the Text, p.8.

Talking about the Story

Ask the children if they can remember:

What colour was the space monster?

What did the space monster have on his head?

Do you think the space monster was a friendly monster?

What did the spaceships do to the monster?

Where did the monster go at the end?

Follow-up Activities

• Draw a Monster Face.

Give each of the children a sheet of paper and four crayons. (red, blue, green, yellow)

Tell the children they must listen very carefully to what you say.

You are going to tell them what to draw and the colours to use.

1 With your green crayon draw a large circle for the monster's head.

2 With your red crayon draw two horns coming out of the top of the monster's head.
Colour these in red.

3 With your yellow crayon draw three eyes for the monster.

4 With your blue crayon give your monster a big open mouth. Colour it in.

5 With your green crayon give your monster a round nose. Colour it in.

6 Choose any of the colours you have and give your monster some spiky hair.

7 Think very hard and give your monster a name. (If possible, the children may like to try and write the name without help. If not, write the name suggested in yellow high-lighter pen and let the child go over this in pencil or black crayon.)

Put all the monsters on the classroom wall for everyone to see.

- Game: "Zap that!"

Divide the children into pairs.

Make a long strip of paper for each child and divide it into ten sections. Let the children number each 'square' up to ten. Tell the children to choose any four squares for their rocket pads and to colour them in. Tell them not to let anyone see which squares they have chosen.

Each child needs four counters.

They are going to try and 'Zap' the rocket pads.

The first child says to his or her neighbour, "I am going to attack your number two."

If this is a rocket pad then the friend must put a counter on that square.

If it is not a coloured square then he or she replies, "I'm very sorry but that was not a rocket pad." The opponent then has a go. The winner is the first to find the opponent's four rocket pads.

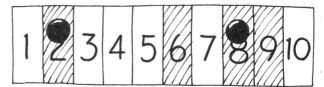

The Train

Introducing the Story

Before reading the story talk to the children about going on a train.

Talk about why people go on trains. Collect as many pictures as possible showing the different kinds of trains. Talk about the different things trains carry, e.g. passengers, freight.

Ask the children:

Have you ever been on a train?

Did the train go fast?

What did you see from the window?

Did you ever go through a tunnel?

Were there lots of people on the train?

Were you going on holiday?

Note: If none of the children have travelled on a train then tell them about a journey you have made.

Reading the Text

See Introduction: Reading the Text, p.8.

Follow-up Activities

- Sing the song:

  Down by the station, early in the morning,
  See the little puffer trains all in a row.
  See the engine driver pull the little handle.
  Choo, choo, choo, and off we go.

(This song can be expanded by the children suggesting other vehicles, e.g. tractor standing in the barn, ship waiting in the harbour, plane sitting on the runway).

- Make a story.

Tell the children that they are going to help you to write a story called 'A train journey'. Start by asking them to suggest who might be going on a train journey. Where do they think this person might be going? Write down what they suggest as fast as necessary.

Craft the story by asking leading questions, e.g. "Would you like to start the story by saying 'One day Mrs So and So wanted to ...', or 'It was the beginning of the holiday. The family were going to go on a train to...'." When the story is complete ask the children to illustrate the different episodes. Write the story in large letters or put it on to the computer.

Finally collect in the illustrations and discuss with the children where they should go in the story. Mount the text and the illustrations on to card or sugar paper and staple the pages together. Read the story to the whole class.

- Letter identification.

  Look at p.10 of the story. Ask the children, "Do you know another word for fast?" Now look at p.16. "Do you know another word for 'Hurry up!'?" Elicit the answer 'quick' or 'quickly'.

  Talk to the children about the letter 'q' and how it is always attached to the letter 'u'.

Ask the children to make the shape of the letters 'qu' in the air. Watch how they form the letters. Give the children a copy of the photocopy master 17.

Before they start to circle the letters read the sentence to them.

- Read the children a story from the "Thomas the Tank Engine" series by Rev W. Awdry (Buzz Books).

The Spaceship

Introducing the Story

Before reading the story ask the children if they can remember the different things they can see in the sky at night. Talk about how people have started to explore space. Tell them about the first men on the moon and what they brought back.

Showing the Story

The aim of this book is to let the children practise the sight vocabulary that they have met in the previous stories. Check with the children that they can identify the different objects that the spaceship is going past: the moon, the planets, the comet, the stars.

Reading the Text

Let the children read the book to you in pairs. As far as possible let them lead the reading.

Encourage them to take the book home and read it to an adult.

Follow-up Activities

- Sing the song: "Off we go."

  Down at the launch pad,
  Early in the morning,
  See us in our spacesuits,
  Standing in a row.
  Climb aboard the spaceship,
  Ready for the take off.
  Zoom, zoom, zoom, and off we go.

- Make a space collage.

  Use large sheets of black sugar paper for the background.

  Ask the children what space objects they would like to make to put on the picture.

Let some of the children make stars from silver paper.

Let some of the children draw a planet on card and colour it, e.g. Mars could be red.

Encourage them to look in a book to see what colours the planets appear to be through the telescope.

Show the children pictures of a comet and ask them how they think they could make one to put on the picture.

Let two children make a spaceship from boxes and card.

Label the drawing using white labels. Mount the picture on the wall.

- Poem: "Twinkle, twinkle little star."

  Twinkle, twinkle little star.
  How I wonder what you are.
  Up above the world so high.
  Like a diamond in the sky.

Letter shapes

QU   qu

R   r

Z   z

17

Name_____

The queen and the duck

The queen wanted to ask the duck a quick question, but all it would say was quack, quack, quack!

Read the sentence, then circle all the qu words and letters.

My Bike Can Fly!

Teaching Points for Set 2 Book 8:

sight words - over under
letter recognition - d f u
focus - positional language

My Bike Can Fly!

Introducing the Story

Before reading the story ask the children:

Have you got a bike?

Can you ride a two-wheeler?

Can a bike fly?

In this story the boy has a rather special bike and it can fly.

The Oral Story-Telling

Jason got on his special flying bike. He said, "I can fly under the trees and over the street. I can fly under the bridge and over the town." Then Jason flew under the helicopter and waved to the pilot. Oh dear, the pilot looks a bit surprised. He has never seen a flying bike before. "Uh oh!" said Jason, " I must fly home fast."

Reading the Text

See Introduction: Reading the Text, p.8.

Talking about the Story

Ask the children:

Can you remember where Jason flew?

He flew ..... the trees and ..... the street.

He flew ..... the bridge and ..... the town.

What do you think the helicopter pilot reported back to the control tower at the airport?

Follow-up Activities

• Sing the song :

When I was one I'd just begun
Going over the sea.

I jumped aboard the ferryman's boat
And the ferryman said to me
"Going over, going under
Stand to attention like a soldier
With a one, two, three."

When I was two I lost a shoe.
When I was three I climbed a tree.
When I was four I found a door.
When I was five I learned to dive.

• Game: "Under and over".

In the hall line the children up into two equal lines. Give each team a tennis ball. The first child in each team passes the ball over his or her head to the child behind. That child passes the ball **under** his or her legs to the next child. That child passes the ball **over**, etc. In this way the ball passes over and under the line until it reaches the child at the back. That child rushes to the front of his or her line and that team sits down to show that they have finished. The first team to sit down is the winner. You can extend the game by repeating it until the person who started at the front is back at the front again.

• Letter recognition.

Read the following lists to the children and ask them to identify the word that begins with the different letter.

Game 1 :

duck,	dirty,	window,	down;
dog,	dagger,	dairy,	bird;
daffodil,	bike,	danger,	dark;
play,	date,	daughter,	day;
dawn,	dear,	drop,	brick.

Game 2 :
under,   umbrella,   trousers,   uncle;
skate,   ugly,   unfair,   unhappy;
unlucky,   important,   until,   upstairs;
upon,   untidy,   inside,   upset.

Game 3 :
fox,   face,   factory,   valley;
fair,   far,   vet,   farm;
fast,   video,   fall,   film;
visitor,   fee,   finish,   fire.

The Rescue Helicopter

Introducing the Story

Before reading the story ask the children:

Have you ever seen a helicopter?

What makes a helicopter different from an aeroplane?

How does a helicopter fly?

There are some special helicopters that are used to rescue people who get into difficulty in the sea or on a mountain. They are called Rescue Helicopters.

Reading the Text

See Introduction: Reading the Text, p.8.

Talking about the Story

Ask the children :

Why did the rescue helicopter go to help the man?

Can you remember where the helicopter flew? (over the airport, over the farm, over the shops, over the sea)

How did the rescue helicopter save the man?

Follow-up Activities

• Give each child a copy of the photocopy master 18 (Activity Book A13). The child should look at the story, choose the right word and write it in the correct space.

• Positional language

Take a small toy helicopter in to school. Position it in various places, e.g. on a book; on a table; beside a book; under the table. Ask the children to say where the helicopter is. As a variation let the children take it in turns to put the helicopter somewhere and then say where it is, e.g. "I have put the helicopter next to the door."

• Read the poem:

The helicopter waits at the airport
Waiting for a call.
Someone needs help out at sea
Or someone's had a fall.

The helicopter waits at the airport
Always ready to go.
Has someone got lost on the mountain
Or is someone stuck in the snow?

The helicopter waits at the airport
It hears the call on the phone
The helicopter's out on a rescue
To bring someone safely home.

• Talk about the RNLI. What do they do? What vehicles do they use? How do they get the money to pay for their rescue operations? If you are near the coast arrange for someone from the RNLI to visit, or visit a lifeboat station with the class.

• Read with the children, "Budgie, the Helicopter" by HRH The Duchess of York (Simon and Schuster).

Letter shapes

D   d

F   f

U   u

Under the Sea

Introducing the Story

Before reading the story ask the children:

What creatures live in the sea?

What is the biggest creature you can think of in the sea?

What is the smallest?

What creatures might chase each other in the sea?

Reading the Text

Encourage children to read as much as possible of this text on their own. They may need help with the word 'chasing'.

Talking about the Story

Some questions to ask:

Can you remember who chased:
the shrimp?
the little fish?
the big fish?
the sea lion?
the shark?
the dolphin?

Did you expect the dolphin to chase the shark away?

Follow-up Activities

- Play games which draw attention to different sizes e.g. ask the children to line up in height order; sort out bricks into size order; use Multi-Link blocks to make constructions which move up in height.

- Make a collage of creatures found in the sea.

- Talk about how people can also be a danger to sea animals such as dolphins, seals and whales - by using large fishing nets and by causing pollution.

- Say the finger rhyme :

Here is the sea, the wavy sea. (Make wave movements with hands.)
Here is the boat and here is me. (Lightly clench fist and pop one finger through for "me".)
All the little fishes down below, (Put hands down low.)
Wriggle their tails, and away they go. (Wriggle fingers then put them behind you.)

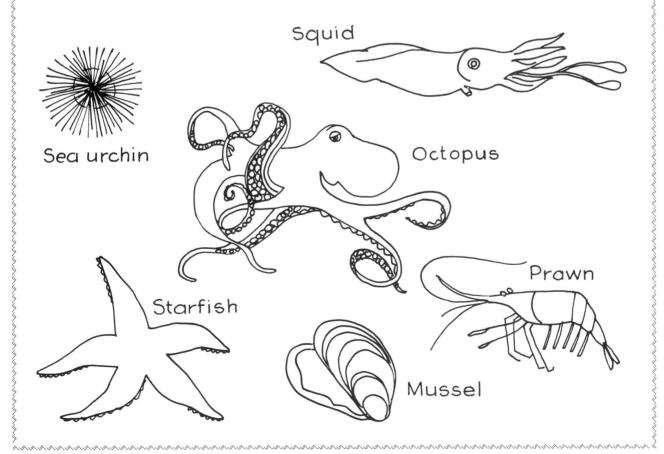

Squid

Sea urchin

Octopus

Starfish

Prawn

Mussel

Fill in the words

over   under

The 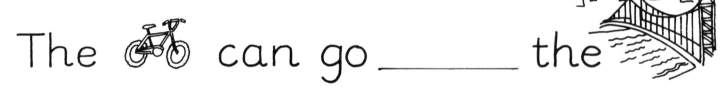 can go _____ the

The can go _____ the

The can go _____ the

The can go _____ the

The can go _____ the

Look at the story and choose the right word. Write it in the space.

The Apple

Teaching Points for Set 2 Book 9:	sight words - is my this letter recognition - i r y focus - colours

The Apple

Introducing the Story

Before reading the story ask the children:

Have you got any brothers and sisters? Are they older or younger than you?

What do you do if they sometimes want something that you also want?

What happens if there is not enough to share between the family?

Have you got any pets?

Do your pets sometimes eat things that they shouldn't?

The Oral Story-Telling

In our garden there was a large apple tree. Some years it had lots of apples on it but some years it only had one or two apples. I can remember one year there was only one apple on the tree.

Every day my Grandfather went out and looked at the apple. "This is my apple," he said and he went back into the house.

Every day my Grandmother went out and out and looked at the apple. "This is my apple," she said and she went back into the house.

Every day my Mum went out into the garden and looked at the apple. "This is my apple," she said and went back into the house.

Every day my Dad went into the garden and looked at the apple. "This is my apple," he said and went into the house.

My sister Ann went into the garden and looked at the apple. "This is my apple," she said and went into the house.

My brother Tom went into the garden and looked at the apple. "This is my apple," he said and he knocked it off the tree.

Who do you think saw the apple? The goat saw the apple. "This is my apple," said the goat and he ate it in one mouthful. CRUNCH!

Reading the Text

See Introduction: Reading the Text, p.8.

Talking about the Story

Ask the children:

Who do you think should have had the apple?

What would you have done if there had only been one apple?

Do you think the goat enjoyed the apple?

What other food does a goat like?

Follow-up Activities

• Bring an apple into the classroom and ask the children to describe it. What colour is it? Does it have a smell? Does it feel rough or smooth? What shape is it?

Cut the apple in half. Talk to the children about the core of the apple and the pips.

If the pips look ripe enough plant them in some pots. Let the children water one pot carefully and leave the other one dry. In which pot do the pips grow?

• Make and illustrate a consequence chart.

Let the children draw some happy faces and some unhappy faces.

Write the sentences below on to the chart leaving enough room to stick the faces at the end.

If we share we will be.....

If we don't share we will be.....

If we are noisy we will be.....

If we are quiet we will all be.....

If we are good we will be .....

If we are naughty we will be.....

If we are kind we will be.....

If we are unkind we will be.....

Ask the children how they feel for each sentence. They should stick a suitable face at the end of each line.

• Talk about parents and grandparents. Explain to the children how their parents were once little children like them. Ask them to ask their parents what it was like when they went to school. Can they remember the books and stories they read?

Ask them to ask their parents if they have any photograph of when they were at school. Show the children photographs of when you were at school.

Talk about their grandparents. Explain that they were once little children who also went to school.

• Read the story of "The Greedy Goat" to the class using the big book version published by Harcourt Brace and Jovanovich.

This Is My Bed

Introducing the Story

Before reading the story ask the children:

Do you know what a clown looks like?

What kind of clothes does a clown wear?

What kind of shoes does a clown wear?

What kind of nose does a clown have?

Do clowns like falling over?

Do clowns like pretending to be sad?

Reading the Text

See Introduction: Reading the Text, p.8.

This story uses many of the sight words from previous books. Let the children read the words 'This is my' and also the 'colour' of the clown.

Follow-up Activities

• Give each child a copy of the photocopy master 19 (Activity Book A14).

Encourage the child to read both the words and the colours.

• Rhyme time:

Let the children supply the missing colour.

This is my bed
And I'm dressed in.....

I'm a good fellow
And I'm dressed in .....

I like to be seen
And I'm dressed in .....

I'm stuck in the glue
And I'm dressed in .....

I'm going to town
And I'm dressed in .....

I'll say goodnight
And I'm dressed in .....

• My Clown.

Give each child a strip of paper. This can be made by cutting a sheet of A4 paper and joining it in the middle. Fold the paper into three sections.

Tell the children to listen carefully to the instructions so that they can each draw a super clown.

On the top fold of paper draw a large circle.
Draw a funny hat on the top.
Draw two round eyes.
Draw a large round nose.
Draw a smiling mouth.

On the second fold of paper draw a body. Make the body go from the top of the fold to the bottom.
Draw three round buttons.
Draw two arms and hands.

On the last fold of paper draw two legs.
Draw two funny shoes.

Colour your clown with lovely bright colours.

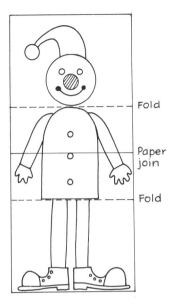

Fold

Paper join

Fold

My Dad

Before Reading the Story

Check that the children in the group have a father either that is at home or one that they do see regularly.

Showing the Story

Ask the children:

What do you think the dad is doing here? (p.18, swimming)

What is the dad doing on this page? (p.19 sailing, then fishing, cooking, reading)

Reading the Text

See Introduction: Reading the Text, p.8.

Talking about the Story

Ask the children:

What do you like doing after school?

What does your Mum like doing?

What does your Dad like doing?

What do your pets like doing?

Follow-up Activities

• Let each child make a chart of things he or she likes to do. They could find pictures from magazines or draw all the things they like to do.

Write the days of the week across the chart:

On Monday I like to (play with my friends).

On Tuesday I like to (visit my gran).

On Wednesday I like to (go swimming).

On Thursday I like to (go shopping with my dad).

On Friday I like to (go to the allotment).

On Saturday I like to (watch T.V.).

On Sunday I like to (play with my sister).

Encourage the children to select one or two things they like doing for each day of the week.

• Show the children the book, "Can't you sleep little bear?" by Martin Waddell (Walker).

Talk about the pictures and read the text with a small group.

Letter shapes

l   i

R   r

Y   y

Write and colour

The red clown said,
"This is my ⬭ nose."

The green clown said,
"_ _ _ _ _  hat."

The yellow clown said,
"_ _ _ _ _ tie."

The brown clown said,
"_ _ _ _ _ belt."

The pink clown said,
"_ _ _ _ _ flower."

The Sausage

By Jillian Cutting
Illustrations by Peter Stevenson

Teaching Points for Set 2 Book 10:

sight words - said the
letter recognition - revision of letters
focus - speech marks

The Sausage

Introducing the Story

Before reading the story ask the children:

What do you like to eat?

This is a story about a sausage that a lot of animals wanted to eat but only one managed it in the end.

The Oral Story-Telling

The giant was cooking his breakfast. He was cooking a big fat sausage. "Yum! Yum!" said the giant, "I like sausages." Just then a cheeky mouse peeped over the table and stole the sausage and said "This is my sausage." As he pushed it off the table a clever cat pounced on it and said, "This is my sausage." As the cat ran out of the door a dog snatched the sausage and said, "This is my sausage." On the road he met a goat. "This is my sausage," said the goat. The goat was just about to eat the sausage when a seagull swooped down and picked it up. As the seagull flew over the sea it dropped the sausage. A big shark came up out of the water, "This is my sausage," he said. So, in the end, neither the giant, nor the mouse, nor the cat, nor the dog, nor the goat, nor the seagull ate the sausage. The shark ate it all up.

Reading the Text

See the Introduction: Reading the Text, p.8.

Talking about the Story

Ask the children to look back through the book to see how, in each picture, there are clues suggesting which animal will steal the sausage next. Then close the book and ask the children if they can remember who had the sausage first, second, third, etc. (giant, mouse, cat, dog, goat, seagull, shark)

Follow-up Activities

• Say the number rhyme: "Ten fat sausages".

Ten fat sausages,
Frying in the pan
One went 'pop'
And the other went 'bang'.

Eight fat sausages,
Frying in the pan.
One went 'pop'
And the other went 'bang'.

Six fat sausages, etc.

• Give each child a copy of the photocopy master 20 (Activity Book A15) and ask them to fill in the right letters for the rhyming words. The pictures provide the clues to the words.

• Make a breakfast book. Draw pictures or use collage to show all the things children like to eat for breakfast. The text below each illustration could be ..... likes to eat ....., with the name of the child and a picture of a chosen breakfast food.

The Tree House

Introducing the Story

Before reading the story ask the children:

Do you know what a tree house is?

Would you like to go in one?

Why would you have to be very careful in a tree house?

Who do you think would like to live in a tree house?

Reading the Text

See the Introduction: Reading the Text, p.8.

Talking about the Story

Ask the children:

Can you remember all the creatures who thought it was their tree house? (owl, bee, bird, squirrel, spider, cat)

Do you think the girl would let them stay in her tree house?

Follow-up Activities

• Say the hand rhyme:

Here is a house built up high, (Stretch arms up touching fingerprints.)

With two tall chimneys reaching the sky. (Stretch arms up separately.)

Here are the windows (Make square shape with hands.)

Here is the door (Knock.)
If we peep inside, we'll see a mouse on the floor.
(Raise hands in fright.)

• Find the rhyme.

Which word rhymes ?

owl	house	tree	outing	towel
bee	tree	house	girl	bike
bird	bike	bee	heard	house
spider	spin	rider	bee	house
cat	cap	can	bee	sat

• Act it out.

Children take the individual animal parts saying in turn :

"Here is my house," says the (t-wit t-woo).
"Here is my house," says the (buzz buzz).
"Here is my house," says the (tweet tweet).
"Here is my house," says the (leaping movements with hands to represent squirrel leaping from branch to branch).
"Here is my house," says the (spread fingers to represent spider descending).
"Here is my house," says the (mee-ow).

• Say the alphabet rhyme:

A B C D	*What can you see?*
D E F G	*I see a tall tree.*
G H I J	*What can you say?*
J K L M	*I can say hem.*
M N O P	*What can you see?*
P Q R S	*I see a nice dress.*
S T U V	*What is for tea?*
V W X Y	*A nice big apple pie.*
Y Z all done	*Let's say it again for fun!*

• Sing the alphabet to the tune of "Twinkle, twinkle little star". If you say the last letter as "Zee" you can add the rounding off lines:
Now I know my ABC. Won't you say it again with me?

• Say this alphabet rhyme:

A B C D	*I know my letters perfectly.*
E F and G	*I can see them all you see.*
H I J K	*I can say them every day.*
L M N O	*The alphabet is good to know.*
P Q and R	*I can say them in the car.*
S T U V	*I can say them having tea.*
W X Y Z	*I even say them in my bed!*

Dinner

Before Reading the Story

Ask the children:

What do you think an elephant (tiger, hippo, monkey, giraffe, crocodile, zookeeper) eats for dinner?

Reading the Text

See Introduction: Reading the Text, p.8.

Talking about the Story

Ask the children:

Who ate the vegetables and dried grass? (elephant, hippo)

Who ate the meat? (tiger)

Who ate the fruit and nuts? (monkey)

Who ate the dried grass and leaves? (giraffe)

Who ate the fish? (crocodile)

Who ate pork chop, potatoes, vegetables, bread roll and cherry pie? (zookeeper)

Follow-up Activities

• Say the rhyme: "What did you have to eat?"

Ask the children to sit in a circle. They all say the first two lines and then take turns in saying what they had to eat around the circle.

What did you have for dinner today?

What did you have to eat?

I had (Child fills in, e.g. pizza and baked potato).

That's what I had to eat.

• Play "I went to dinner."

The first child says, "I went to dinner and I had (e.g. a potato). The next child says, "I went to dinner and I had a potato and (e.g. a piece of cheese), and so on with each child trying to remember the things in order which the children before them have had.

• Read to the children the story, "Mog at the Zoo" by Helen Nicoll & Jan Pienkowski (Heinemann).

• Share with the children the book, "Dear Zoo" by Rod Campbell (Picture Puffin).

• Let the children read with you the Sunshine book, "Dinner" (Heinemann).

Fill in the letters

A _ish on a _ish

A _oat in a _oat

A _ee in a _ree

A _at on a _at

A _nake on a _ake

A _et in a _et

A _at in a _at

A _an on a _an

A _ing with a _ing

A _rog on a _og

Fill in the missing letters.

Jack and the Giant

Jack and the Giant

By Joy Cowley
Illustrations by Korky Paul

Teaching Points for Set 3 Book 1:	sight words - down went letter recognition - sh focus - size

Jack and the Giant

Introducing the Story

Before reading the story ask the children to think about giants:

Where do you think they live?

How big do you think they are?

Are they kind or cruel?

Where do they get their clothes from?

Would you like to meet a giant?

What would you say to a giant?

The Oral Story-Telling

Jack was always getting into trouble and do you know why?

He just couldn't stop exploring. Even when he was told that he must stay near his home and behave, do you know what he did? He decided to climb up a tall beanstalk that was growing near to the house and just see what he could see. Just in case there was somewhere to explore.

Well, up he climbed and what do you think he saw? Not too far away was a large castle. It belonged to a giant. Jack soon set off to the giant's house. He went up the giant's path. He went up the giant's steps and then he crawled under the giant's door.

He was frozen. "I am cold," said Jack "I want a hot bath." Just then he saw something on the top of an enormous table and steam was rising from it. "That will soon warm me up," thought Jack so he climbed on to the giant's table. Just at that moment the giant opened the door and came in. "GET OUT OF MY SOUP" he roared.

Jack was surprised. He was just having a lovely hot bath. "I thought my bath had a lovely smell," he said!

Reading the Text

See Introduction: Reading the Text, p.8.

Talking about the Story

Ask the children:

Do you think Jack was silly or sensible to take a bath?

Why was Jack cold?

How do you think Jack felt when he saw the giant?

What did the giant say when he saw Jack?

What do you think the giant did with the soup? Did he give Jack some?

Follow-up Activities

• Read the class a version of the story, "Jack and the Bean Stalk".

• Read the class, "Zerelda's Ogre" by Tomi Ungerer (Magnet).

• Give a copy of the photocopy master 21 to each child. Ask the children to talk to a partner or group about size and how you order things according to size. Use the terms big, bigger, biggest; small, smaller, smallest.

• Decide on a menu for a giant. Talk to the group about starters, main meals and puddings.

Read them the story, "Zerelda's Ogre" again and ask which meal they would have given the ogre?

Collect from the children all the things they would offer on the menu. Sort out the items into the three categories. (starters, main course, pudding).

Help the children to write and illustrate each item. When they have completed this, arrange their 'food' on to a giant piece of paper for the menu.

The Chase

Introducing the Story

Before reading the text ask the children:

Why is it dangerous to run on a road?

Do you know how fast a car is allowed to go on a road?

What happens if a car is caught speeding?

Do you think animals know that roads are dangerous?

Reading the Text

See Introduction: Reading the Text, p.8.

Talking about the Story

Some questions to ask:

What excuses do you think the animals gave to the traffic officer?

What addresses might the animals have given?

What do you think the traffic officer said to the animals?

What punishment would she have given to the animals?

Who do you think had to pay each of the following:

three slices of cheese?

two handfuls of corn?

five old bones?

two bundles of hay?

£20.00.

Follow-up Activities

• Read the class a version of the story of "The Gingerbread Boy".

Ask the questions:

Which parts of the stories are similar?

How are the endings different?

Which story do you prefer? Why?

Which story do you think was written first?

• Read the class the story of "The King, the Mice and the Cheese," by Nancy and Eric Gurney (Collins).

How is this story similar?

Where is it different?

Which story do you think is the most exciting?

• Write a story.

Using the children in the group who have read the story of "The Chase" help them to write a similar story about themselves. This could be a chase around the playground, or an accumulation of children who are sent with a message to the headteacher.

When the children have decided upon their version of the story give each child one page of the story to write and illustrate. It may be necessary to help them with some spellings. Ask the group to suggest what letters they think the different words begin with and write the words on to a board or large sheet of paper.

Finally mount the pages on to larger sheets of paper or card and help the group to make a cover from stiff card. This book could then become part of the book corner.

When I Went Shopping...

Introducing the Story

Before reading the story with the group ask the children:

Where do you go shopping to get food?

What food do you like to see in the shopping basket?

What sort of food do you think a monster might buy?

What do you think the shop assistants would say if they saw a monster in the shop?

Can you count up to ten?

Can you count backwards from ten?

Reading the Text

See Introduction: Reading the Text, p.8.

Talking about the Story

Ask the children:

How many apples did the monster buy?

How many chocolate bars did the monster buy?

How many buns did the monster buy?

How many cookies did the monster buy?

How many legs of chicken did the monster buy? Beefburgers? Juice? Ice creams? Pizzas?

Why do you think the monster had a sore stomach?

Write the answers on the board. Ask the children to suggest items that they would like to have in these quantities, and put their suggestions next to those of the monster's.

Follow-up Activities

• Hear the sound.

Show the children the two letters 'sh' and let them say the sound with you.

Tell them that you are going shopping and that you will give your shopping to the person who listens very carefully. Every time they hear the sound 'sh' in the shopping list they are to put up their hand. If they are correct they can have a counter. The winner is the child with the most counters at the end of the shopping spree.

(The following items could be offered among the list: shampoo, shark, shawl, shears, shed, sheep, sheet, shelf, shells, shields, ships, shirts, shoes, shorts, shovel, shrimps.)

• Game: "I went shopping and I bought".

Each child suggests one item they would like and adds it to the suggestions of the previous players, e.g. I went shopping and I bought one potato.

I went shopping and I bought one potato and two cars.

I went shopping and I bought one potato, two cars and a woolly hat, etc.

See how far the group can remember the items. Can they get up to ten in a row?

• Sing the Song: "Five currant buns".

There were five currant buns in a baker's shop,
Round and fat with sugar on the top.
Along came (child's name) *with a penny one day,*
Bought a currant bun and took it away.

There were four currant buns in a baker's shop,
Round and fat, etc.

• Read to the class, "Grandma goes shopping" by R. and D. Armitage (Picture Puffin).

21 Name_____

_____

Big, bigger, biggest

big

_____

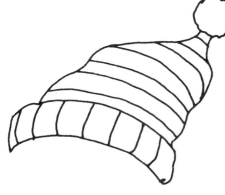

biggest

_____

bigger

_____   _____   _____

Label pictures according to size. Colour the picture.

The Cow in the Hole

The Cow in the Hole

By Joy Cowley
Illustrations by Jan van der Voo

Teaching Points for Set 3 Book 2:	**sight words - get out we will** **letter recognition - th** **focus - speech marks**

The Cow in the Hole

Introducing the Story

Before reading the story ask the children:

Have you ever visited a farm?

What animals did you see on the farm?

Have you seen cows and calves in a field?

What do you think cows like to eat?

The Oral Story-Telling

I know some farmers who had a beautiful herd of Friesian cows. They were very proud of them and this is the story about a funny thing that happened to one of the cows. She fell down a hole!

Well, she mooed and mooed and soon the farmers heard her. "We will get you out," they said and they pushed and pushed but the cow did not get out.

Some policemen were near and they ran over to see what was happening. "We will get you out," said the policemen and they pushed and pushed but the cow did not get out. Along came some firefighters. "We will get you out," they said and they pushed and pushed but the cow did not get out.

Then along came some children and what do you think they had got with them? They had large bundles of hay. "We will get you out," said the children and they held out the hay to the cow. Well she loved hay, so what did she do? She climbed out of the hole. "Hurrah!" shouted everyone and the children danced round the cow.

What did the cow do? She ate the hay, of course.

Reading the Text

See Introduction: Reading the Text, p.8.

Talking about the Story

Ask the children:

What do you think the farmer said to the children?

What do you think the policemen said?

If a horse fell into a hole how would you try to get him out?

If a lion fell in a hole how would you try to get him out?

Follow-up Activities

• How would you entice the following out of a hole:

a cow (hay); a rabbit (lettuce); a mouse (cheese); a bird (bread crumbs); a monkey (banana); a donkey, (carrots); me ?

• What do you think? True or false?

Say the following sentences and ask the children to say if they think they could be true or unlikely?

The boat went slowly down the road.

The cow munched the green grass.

The car climbed up the lamp post.

The tree grew as high as a house.

The mouse ran into his hole.

The hedgehog rolled up into a sandwich.

• Letter search.

Give each child a page from a magazine or a newspaper and a highlighter pen or crayon. Ask the children to try and find every time the letters 'th' occur together in a word. They mark these with the pen. Let the children count up and see which of them had the most 'th's on their sheet. Encourage the children to make the sound 'th' when they spot one.

- Speech bubble writing.

  Give each child a copy of the photocopy master 22 (Activity Book B1). Talk with them about the words they think should go into the speech bubbles. Encourage them to try to write the words without help from you.

- Singing game: "The Farmer in the Dell".

  The farmer in the dell,
  The farmer in the dell,
  Heigh-ho, the derry-o,
  The farmer in the dell.

  The farmer takes a wife, etc.
  The wife takes a child, etc.
  The child takes a nurse, etc.
  The nurse takes a dog, etc.
  The dog takes a cat, etc.
  The cat takes a rat, etc.
  The rat takes the cheese, etc.
  The cheese stands alone, etc.

  The children form a circle with one child as the 'farmer' in the middle. They join hands and sing while dancing around the farmer.

At the end of the first verse, the farmer chooses someone as his wife, and so on. On the last verse the child chosen as the cheese must stand by him or herself and can then be the farmer for a following game.

- Song: "Old MacDonald had a farm, E,I,E,I,O".

  Old MacDonald had a farm,
  E,I,E,I,O.
  And on this farm he had a dog,
  E,I,E,I,O.
  With a bow-wow here, and a bow, wow there,
  Here a bow, there a bow, everywhere a bow-wow,
  Old MacDonald had a farm,
  E,I,E,I,O.
  And on this farm he had some ducks, chicks, cows, pigs, etc.

  This is a cumulative song with all the farmyard animals and their sounds being named each time.

- Read the poem, "The Cow" from "A Child's Garden of Verses" by Robert Louis Stevenson (Heinemann).

- Read the class the story, "The cow who fell into the canal" by Phyllis Krasilovky (World's Work).

The Animal Clinic

Introducing the Story

Before reading the story ask the children:

   What happens to you when you go to a clinic?

   Have you been to a doctor?

   What did the doctor do?

   Who do you take sick animals to see?

Reading the Text

See Introduction: Reading the Text, p.8.

Talking about the Story

Ask the children:

   Why do you think the animals said they were better?

   Can you remember who had a sore throat?

Can you remember who had a sore nose? Tooth? Stomach?

Who did the animals decide to go and see?

Was this a good idea?

Follow-up Activities

- What's wrong with me?

  Say the following rhymes and ask the children to complete the missing word.

  Doctor, doctor, help me please,
  I have fallen and cut my .....

  Doctor, doctor, please come quick.
  I am feeling very .....

  Doctor, doctor, I'm in bed,
  I have fallen and bumped my ...

  Doctor, doctor, please don't go,
  I have fallen and stubbed my .....

Doctor, doctor, please come here,
I have fallen and hurt my .....

• Let's Find Out.

Using a reference book or a Guinness Book of Records, see if you and the children can find out:

Which is the tallest animal?

Which is the fastest animal?

Which is the heaviest animal?

Which is the fiercest animal?

Which is the slowest animal?

Try to help the children devise some more questions to ask.

When the answers have been found put the answers up on a classroom wall, or make a chart of the information.

• Read to the class the story, "Chicken Little" retold by Stephen Kellogg (Hutchinson).

The Sauce in the Bottle

Introducing the Story

Before reading the story ask the children:

Do you like putting sauce on your food?

What is your favourite sauce?

What food do you put sauce on?

Have you ever found it difficult to open the bottle?

Have you ever found it difficult to shake the sauce out of the bottle?

Reading the Text

See Introduction: Reading the Text, p.8.

Talking about the Story

Ask the children:

What do you think Dad said when the sauce came out of the bottle?

What do you think Mum said when the sauce came out of the bottle?

Do you think everyone was pleased when the sauce came out?

Do you think Ben ate all the sauce that was on his food?

Follow-up Activities

• Rhyme:

*Shake and shake the ketchup bottle
None will come and then a lot will!*

• Shake the word off the end of the sentence.

Explain to the children that they are going to 'lose' a word off the end of the sentence each time they say it.

Shake, shake, shake the sauce, put it on your supper.

Shake, shake, shake the sauce, put it on your ...

Shake, shake, shake the sauce, put it on ...

...

Continue until no words are left!

Sometimes the children find it easier to clap the missing words.

• Read to the class the story, "Mrs Pig's Bulk Buy" by Mary Rayner (Picturemac).

Fill in the words

The farmer said,
"I will get you out."

The policeman said,
"I will get you out."

The firefighter said,
"I will get you out."

The girl said,
"Here is some hay."

Write what each person says in the speech bubble.

The Speed Boat

The Speed Boat

By Jillian Cutting
Illustrations by Jennifer Lautusi

Teaching Points for Set 3 Book 3:

sight words - past went
letter recognition - sp
focus - use of bold typeface

The Speed Boat

Introducing the Story

Before reading the story ask the children:

Have you been on a boat?

What different kinds of boat can you think of?

How fast can boats go?

If you go on a boat what must you wear in case you fall in the water?

What must boats be careful to avoid?

The Oral Story-Telling

This is a story about four naughty children. One day they went out in their parents' speed boat. At first they went slowly but soon they decided to go as fast as they could. They raced past some children who were swimming. "Look out!" shouted the swimmers but the children took no notice. They raced past some windsurfers. "Look out!" shouted the windsurfers and one fell in the water. The children took no notice. They were having fun. They went past some rowers and then past some divers. "Look out!" shouted the rowers and the divers but the children took no notice. The speed boat raced past some yachts. "Look out. Look out for the rocks!" shouted the sailors, but the children took no notice. What do you think happened? Their boat crashed on the rocks and a big hole was made in the side. Now the children were not so happy. Who do you think came to help them?

Reading the Text

See Introduction: Reading the Text, p.8.

Talking about the Story

Ask the children:

Who do you think helped the children in the boat?

What do you think they said to the children?

What would you have said?

What do you think the children said to their parents?

Do you think they will be allowed in the boat again?

Follow-up Activities

• Sing the song with the children:

We are on a speed boat,
Going very fast.
"Look out," said the swimmers/
windsurfers/rowers/divers/ sailors.
But we raced on past.

• Encourage the children to listen to and identify the sound for the blend 'sp'.

Ask them to tell you the words that start with the sound 'sp' from the following:

speed,	spear,	book;
speck,	swan,	speak;
sink,	spaniel,	spot;
spider,	spoon,	string;
splash,	spin,	pin;
spy,	pie,	spill.

• Up or down?

Ask the children, "Which do you think will float and which will sink?"

Boat? Windsurfer? Stones? Plastic? Wood? Coins? Sand?

This could be followed up by testing some classroom objects in a bowl of water.

• Read the story, "The Lighthouse Keeper's Lunch" by R. and D. Armitage (Puffin).

My Tooth

Introducing the Story

Before reading the story ask the children:

Has anyone got a loose tooth?

Has anyone already lost a tooth?

How did it come out?

What will you do with your tooth when it comes out?

Reading the Text

See Introduction: Reading the Text, p.8.

Talking about the Story

Ask the children:

Would you let anyone pull out your tooth?

If you had to choose one way which would you choose?

Who do you go and see who keeps a check on your teeth?

Follow-up Activities

• Play: "Would you rather...?"

Ask the children to choose from the following:

Would you rather pull out your tooth or take a lion for a walk?

Would you rather pull out your tooth or sing a song in assembly?

Would you rather pull out your tooth or have your hair washed?

Would you rather pull out your tooth or put your hand in a crocodile's mouth?

Would you rather pull out your tooth or stand in the rain for ten minutes?

Would you rather pull out your tooth or walk through a deep puddle?

• Read the book, "Would you rather?" by John Burningham (Picture Lions).

• If there is a child who has not given a milk tooth to the tooth fairy he or she might be persuaded to allow you to place the tooth in a glass of Cola and watch what happens.

• Read to the children "Going to the Dentist" by S. Cartwright (Usborne Books).

• Make a poster: These things are good for my teeth/These things are not good for my teeth.

Ask the children to cut out pictures from magazines or to bring in wrappers from food items to put into the right space. Discuss with the children where to place each wrapper, i.e. Is it good for one's teeth or not?

My teeth

These things are good for my teeth.

These things are not good for my teeth.

Reading

Introducing the Story

Before reading the story ask the children:

What do you like to read about the most?

Giants/ monsters/dinosaurs?

Horses/ crocodiles/ monkeys?

Ghosts/ magicians/dragons?

Frogs/ dogs/ kittens?

Sun/moon/ stars?

Reading the Text

See Introduction: Reading the Text, p.8.

Follow-up Activities

• Make a list of the titles of all the stories the group can remember reading.

Ask the children:

Do you have a favourite book?

Why do you like it?

Give each child a copy of the photocopy master 23 to complete. Talk about favourite stories, books and authors.

Discuss with the children what they would like to write in the blank boxes. They may also colour in the box with their favourite statement - looking at books, listening to stories, or reading with a friend.

• Let the children choose a book to display in the book corner.

Let them write their name on small pieces of card to stand in front of their book.

Encourage them to write both first and surnames on the cards. Very often the surname gets overlooked!

• Make a 'Big Book' with the group.

Ask each child what they like reading about the most.

Let each child draw a book, or give them an outline to colour, and write on it the thing they most like reading about.

Write on to large sheets of paper, "(Child's name) likes reading about..." and stick his/her picture under a flap so that other children have to guess before they are shown the answer.

Make a firm cover for the book and place it in the book corner with the children's display.

• Let the children read with you the Sunshine book, "I am a bookworm" (Heinemann).

• Read with the class, "A Bedtime Story" by Mem Fox (Bookshelf, Stanley Thornes).

I like

I like stories about

_____

My favourite author is

_____

_____

I like looking at books

I like listening to stories

I like reading with a friend

My favourite book is

_____

_____

Fill in the blanks with any answers and sentences about reading.

The Penguins

Teaching Points for Set 3 Book 4:

sight words - go   have what
letter recognition - tr
focus - non-fiction

The Penguins

Introducing the Text

Before reading the story ask the children:

Is a penguin a bird, a fish, or an insect?

Have you ever seen a penguin?

Where did you see it?

Do you think penguins like hot or cold countries?

Do you know any other birds that can't fly?

What do you think penguins like to eat?

What enemies do you think a penguin might have?

Setting the Scene

As this is a non-fiction text it is necessary to try to get children to understand some of the differences between fiction and non-fiction and therefore an oral telling is less applicable.

With this text spend time talking to the children about the use of photographs and how the cover of the book gives us a good idea that this could be either a true story or it could be a book about penguins and how they live.

If possible support this text with other non-fiction books and show the children photographs of other types of penguin.

Talk about the size of penguins and how they manage to live in such cold places.

Spend time going through the pictures asking the children what they are learning about the penguins from the pictures. Talk about the reflections in the water and how thick the ice is.

Show the children a globe and explain to them the two cold regions of our world. It might be possible to explain the differences between the Arctic and the Antarctic. One is land surrounded by ice, the other is ice surrounded by land.

Talk about the different animals that live in the different polar regions: Antarctic - king penguin, fur seal, Weddell seal, killer whale, blue whale, crab-eater seal, cormorant, octopus and squid; Arctic - polar bear, arctic fox, killer whale, caribou, wolves, snowy owl.

Reading the Text

See Introduction: Reading the Text, p.8.

Talking about the Text

Ask the children:

Why do the penguins walk on the ice?

Why do the penguins slide on the ice?

What do the penguins want to find in the water?

Who found the penguins?

What did the penguins do?

What other animals could the killer whales eat?

Follow-up Activities

• Make a collage of life in the Antarctic. Use a sheet of blue paper and draw a line to separate land from sea. Explain to the children that they are going to show a cross-section through the land and sea so that they can show animals that live below the sea as well as on land.

Use thick raised white wall paper and cut out large icebergs. Position them so that about $5/6$ is below sea-level.

Using black paper let the children cut out penguins, colour their front white, and add yellow feet. Ask the children, "What other animals and fish might you see?" Let them cut these out and place them on the picture. Finally let each child label the different parts of the collage.

• Rhyme: "One little penguin".

One little penguin swimming in the sea,
Said to the killer whale, "You can't catch me."

Two little penguins playing in the snow,
Said to the killer whale, "Off you go."

Three little penguins riding on a wave,
Said to the killer whale, "We're so brave."

Four little penguins playing near the ice,
"Mmmm," said the killer whale, "You look nice."

Five little penguins swimming far away,
Escaped from the killer whale to live another day.

• Making a walking penguin.

Give each child a copy of an outline of a penguin. Let the children colour their penguins and cut out the holes for their feet. They can walk their penguins by putting two fingers through the holes.

Holes for fingers

Trucks

Introducing the Text

Before reading the text to the children ask them:

What things do you think a truck can carry?

How many wheels does a truck have? (Accept any reasonable answer.)

Do trucks travel fast or slowly?

What kind of roads do you find lots of trucks on?

What other vehicles are used to carry lots of people and goods?

Reading the Text

See Introduction: Reading the Text, p.8.

After Reading the Text

Ask the children:

How many different trucks can you remember?

Which truck do you think was the largest?

Can a truck carry a truck?

Which truck would you most like to see?

Follow-up Activities

• Sing with the children: "The wheels on the truck go round and round." See p. 159 (Set 4 Book 8).

• Where did your truck go?

Let the children work in pairs.

Give each child a copy of the photocopy master 24.

Tell one child to draw a line from the truck to the depot.

Then this child must tell his or her friend how to get the truck to the depot without showing the friend the route drawn. The friend should draw in the route on his or her own sheet, as it is described.

When the truck is in the depot let the children compare routes.

The second child could use a different coloured crayon and draw a different route and this time he or she tells the partner how to get to the depot.

• Rhyme: "What's my load?"

I am a truck
Going down the road.

I've been to the brickyard.
So what's my load?

I am a truck
Going down the road.
I've been to the fruit farm
So what's my load?

I am a truck
Going down the road.
I've been to the coal mine
So what's my load?

I am a truck
Going down the road.
I've been to the supermarket
So what's my load?

- Make a truck book.

  Give each child a rectangle of card.

  Tell the child to colour the card and write his or her name on it.

  Draw an outline of a truck on to a sheet of paper leaving a space for the rectangle to fit on to the back of it.

  Let each child write along the bottom of the page, "What have I got?"

  Stick the rectangle 'container' on the truck so that it makes a flap.

Under the rectangle the child can either write or draw the contents of the container.

Make all the sheets into a class book and bind or staple inside a stiff card cover.

- Listen to the sound.

  Write the letters 'tr' and 'bl' on the board.

  Divide the group into two teams.

  Ask a child to come up to the board and give him or her a piece of chalk. Say a word that begins with either 'tr' or 'bl' to the child. The child listens hard and then ticks the sound under the letters that she or he thinks the word begins with.

  A child from the second team comes up to the board. Give him or her a different coloured piece of chalk and a word from the list below. The team with the most ticks wins.

  Some examples of words to use: truck, train, treasure, tree, treat, try, tractor, tray, triangle, black, blade, blank, blow, blind, blouse, blunt, blackberry. If this is too easy try asking the children to distinguish between 'tr' and 'ch', e.g. chain, champion, change, charm, chart, cheap, cherry, chimp, chip, chocolate.

Moving House

Introducing the Story

Before reading the story talk with the children about moving house.

Talk about the good things about moving house. (making new friends, going to a new school, having new places to explore)

Talk about the sad things about moving house. (leaving friends and neighbours, things not fitting in the new rooms, not knowing your way around)

Reading the Text

See Introduction: Reading the Text, p.8.

After reading the story ask the children:

Did the children like their new house?

Who carried the furniture down the stairs?

Do you think it is difficult to move all the furniture?

Can you remember what the men carried down the stairs?

Follow-up Activities

- Play: "I'm moving house".

  Each child takes it in turns to add to the things she or he would take when moving house.

  I'm moving house and I'm taking my bed.

  I'm moving house and I'm taking my bed and my teddy.

  I'm moving house and I'm taking my bed, my teddy and my playhouse, etc.

- Can you pack a box?

  Give the child a box, about the size of a shoe box, and some classroom objects. Can the child pack them all into the box, e.g. bricks, paper, toy, shoe, book?

- Read the story, "Moving Molly" by Shirley Hughes (Bodley Head).

- Read the Sunshine History story, "Moving Day" by Jane Shuter and Fiona Reynoldson (Heinemann).

Name_____

_____

Where did your truck go?

Draw a line from your truck to the depot.

Tell your friend how you got to the depot. What did you drive past?

The Snow Race

The Snow Race
By Jill Eggleton
Illustrations by Tracey Moroney

Teaching Points for Set 3 Book 5:	**sight words - put will your**
	letter recognition - cl
	focus - healthy living

The Snow Race

Introducing the Story

Before reading the story ask the children:

What do you need if you want to go skiing?

What do you wear on your head?

What do you wear on your feet?

What is covering the ground?

The Oral Story-Telling

One day Jan and her dad were on the ski slopes. "I will race you over the snow," said Dad. "I will race you to the shop." Dad put on his skis and Jan put on her skis. "Ready, Steady, Go!" The race had started. Dad went down the hill. Jan followed him down the hill. Dad swerved and went around a rock. Jan swerved and went around the rock. Dad was just about to win the race when "Splat!" He crashed straight into a snowman. Jan swerved past the snowman and went into the shop. Jan had won the race.

Reading the Text

See Introduction: Reading the Text, p.8.

Talking about the Story

Some questions to ask:

Who did you think would win the race?

Could you beat your mum or dad at anything? (running, climbing)

What did Dad and Jan both avoid? (the rock)

What did Dad crash into? (the snowman)

What do you think Dad said when he eventually met Jan in the shop?

Follow-up Activities

• Tell the children the story of "The Tortoise and the Hare". Round off the story with the rhyme:

You all know the story of the tortoise and the hare.
The tortoise took his time but he got there.

• Game: "The Word Race".

Give each child a copy of the photocopy master 25 (Activity Book B2).

Play the game with a partner. You will need a die and six counters each. Throw the die in turns. Look at the row next to the number you have thrown. Find the odd word out. Put a counter on that word. The winner is the first to have a counter in each row.

• Rhyme: "Racing down the mountain".

Racing down the mountain
Speeding across the snow.
Of course, I am in the lead,
I've only a mile to go.

Racing down the mountain,
My skis are going fast.
Of course, I am in the lead,
So at least I won't be last.

Racing down the mountain,
No-one's ahead of me.
Of course, I am in the lead,
Now, what's that shape I see?

Sitting on the mountain,
Everyone's ahead of me.
Of course, I am last of all.
I bumped into a tree!

The Clowns

Introducing the Story

Before reading the story ask the children:

What do clowns wear? (baggy pants, funny hats, red noses)

Where might you see some clowns?

Do clowns do clever things or silly things?

Reading the Text

See Introduction: Reading the Text, p.8.

Talking about the Story

Ask the children:

Where did the clowns put their clown pants? (on their heads)

Where did the clowns put their clown hats? (on their noses)

Where did the clowns dance? (on the table)

What happened?

Follow-up Activities

• Listen to the sound.

Listen carefully to the words and when you hear a word that begins 'cl' then clap your hands.

heads,	clock,	your,	put;
not,	hats,	climb,	big;

noses,	shoes,	dance,	clown;
table,	race,	cloud,	snow;
shop,	clean,	hill,	went;
clever,	rock,	into,	put;
said,	no,	clear,	silly.

• Say the following tongue-twisters:

Clever clowns climb cliffs when it is clear or cloudy.

Clean clowns clatter clocks clumsily.

• Read to the class, "How Do I Put It On?" by Shigeo Wanatabe (Picture Puffin).

• Say the rhyme:

Old (fill in boy's name) *lost his cap.*
He couldn't find it anywhere poor old chap.
He walked down the High Street and everybody said,
"Silly .... you've got it on your head!"

Old (fill in girl's name) *lost her hat.*
She couldn't find it anywhere and that was that.
She walked down the High Street and everybody said,
"Silly .... you've got it on your head!"

• Using face paints let the children paint their friends' faces into clowns. You will need to make sure that no child who is to be painted has a sensitive skin or an allergy to make-up.

Shopping

Introducing the Story

Before reading the story ask the children:

Do you ever go to the supermarket with your mum or dad?

Do you always want to buy the same things as they do?

Do you sometimes ask for something you have seen advertised on T.V.?

Reading the Text

See Introduction: Reading the Text, p.8.

Talking about the Story

Ask the children:

Who wanted the following things: bread (Mum); jellybabies (Lester); popcorn (Lester); butter (Mum); chocolate (Lester); spinach (Mum); onions (Mum); biscuits (Lester)?

Which things would you prefer?

Do you think Mum let Lester keep the things he chose?

Why do you think so?

Follow-up Activities

• Make a big book about healthy eating.

Talk to the children about foods that are good for you and foods that you should not eat too much of. They can draw pictures or cut pictures out from magazines to illustrate the book. Use headings such as: These foods taste nice. These foods are good for you. We shouldn't eat too much of these.

• Game: "Granny went to market and she bought....."

Each child adds to the list of the child before her or him. Encourage the children to add to the list food items that represent healthy eating.

• Using the story talk about different kinds of writing - the same letters looking different and being written in different ways. Some notices are all in big (capital) letters, some are a mixture.

Talk about how different things cost different amounts of money.

• Set up a shop in the classroom. Children can bring in empty packets for the shelves and take it in turn to be the shop-keeper or the customer. Develop a role-playing story with different customers coming in for different things to the shop.

Food		
These foods taste nice.	These foods are good for you.	We should not eat too much of these.

Name_____
_____

Odd one out

The Word Race

6	now	snow	snow
5	went	went	sent
4	down	town	down
3	pat	put	put
2	you	you	your
1	hill	will	will

Play with a partner. Throw the dice. Look at the row next to the number you have thrown. Find the odd one out. Put a counter on that word. First to have a counter on each row wins.

The Sky Diver

The Sky Diver

By Jill Eggleton
Illustrations by Astrid Matijasevic

Teaching Points for Set 3 Book 6:	sight words - down over see went letter recognition - sk focus - positional language - over down into

The Sky Diver

Introducing the Story

Before reading the story ask the children:

Have you ever seen anyone using a parachute?

What does it do?

What do you think sky divers do?

Would you like to try it?

Where would be a soft place to land?

The Oral Story-Telling

One day a sky diver jumped out of an aeroplane. He looked down from the sky and he could see the land far below. He pulled the rip cord and opened his parachute. He started to glide gently down. He looked for a safe place to land. "I can see the river. I will not land there," he said. He saw a cowshed and some cows. "Oh no, I will not land there," he said. He saw a barbed wire fence. "Oh no! I will not land there." He went down, down, down. He saw a tree. "Help!" he said, but he landed in the tree. The birds in the tree were amazed to see a creature coming down from the sky. "Help!" they said, "It's a monster."

Reading the Text

See Introduction: Reading the Text, p.8.

Talking about the Story

Ask the children:

What did the sky diver see as he floated down to earth? (river, cowshed and cows, barbed wire fence, tree)

What would happen if he landed in the river? On the cowshed? The fence?

Follow-up Activities

• Give each child a copy of the photocopy master 26 (Activity Book B3).

Ask the children to choose one of the words listed to fill the gap in each sentence. They should use each word once.

• What Can I See?

I am looking down from the sky. I can see a big building. I can see lots of children. What can I see? (a school)

I am looking down from the sky. I can see fields. I can see animals in a yard. I can see a tractor. What can I see? (a farm)

I am looking down from the sky. I can see a wide road. I can see lots of cars and lorries. They are going very fast. What can I see? (a motorway)

I am looking down from the sky. I can see some water. I can see lots of children playing. I can see some sandcastles. What can I see? (seaside/beach)

• Game: "Snap".

Make 20 small cards with the blends learned so far.

Write a blend on each card.

(10 x 'sk'; 2 x 'sh'; 2 x 'th'; 2 x 'sp'; 2 x 'tr'; 2 x 'cl'.)

Two players are needed for this game. Shuffle the cards and deal them out between the two players. They may SNAP only when 'sk' matches.

(Alternatively, they may play Pelmanism with the cards.)

Ostrich

Introducing the Story

Before reading the story ask the children:

Have you ever seen an ostrich?

Where did you see it?

Have you ever seen an ostrich in a cartoon? How did you know it was an ostrich?

What makes an ostrich different from lots of other birds?

Reading the Text

See Introduction: Reading the Text, p.8.

Talking about the Story

Ask the children:

Can you remember where the ostrich ran first? (fruit shop)

What did he knock over?

What happened when he ran into the restaurant?

What happened when he ran into the street?

Follow-up Activities

• Poem: "Olly, the Ostrich".

*Olly the Ostrich
Ran away from the zoo.
He ran into a fruit shop
And what did he do?*

*Olly the Ostrich
Ran away from the zoo.
He ran into a restaurant
And what did he do?*

*Olly the Ostrich
Went back to the zoo.
He ran into his cage
And a good thing too!*

• Draw a large outline of an ostrich. Let each child draw around his or her hand on to newspaper and then cut out the hand shape. (The ostrich body feathers will need about 20 'hands'.) Stick these on to the outline body of the ostrich. Make the tail feathers by cutting large feather shapes from newspaper and cutting up to the 'spine' of the feathers.

Stick these on to the outline drawing.

• Read to the class, "Why Can't I Fly?" by Ken Brown (Andersen Press).

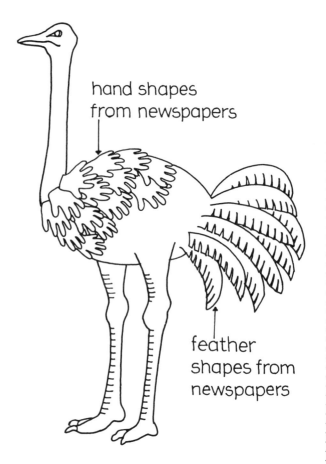

hand shapes from newspapers

feather shapes from newspapers

112

The Giant's Dinner

Introducing the Story

Before reading the story ask the children:

What do you think a giant eats for dinner?

How many potatoes do you think he would eat?

How many chops?

How many peas?

How much gravy?

Reading the Text

See Introduction: Reading the Text, p.8.

Talking about the Story

Ask the children:

What did the giant do with the bones?

What did the giant do with the bread?

What did the cook say to the giant?

What do you think the dog said?

Follow-up Activities

• Make a giant menu for the giant.

Discuss with the children what might be on the menu. Talk about a Starter, a Main Course and a Pudding. Ask each child to draw something they think the giant would like to eat.

Write the menu on to a long strip of paper. Let the children cut out and stick on their drawings round the edge of the menu. Display on the wall.

• Say the Nursery Rhyme: "Old Mother Hubbard".

Old Mother Hubbard, she went to the cupboard,
To fetch her poor dog a bone.
When she got there the cupboard was bare,
And so the poor dog had none.

• Rhyme: "I am a giant".

I am a giant
As tall as a tree
There is no one
Taller than me.

I am a giant
As big as a tree
There is no one
Bigger than me.

I am a giant
As broad as a tree.
There is no one
Broader than me.

I am a giant
As large as a tree.
There is no one
Larger than me.

I am a giant
As tall as a house.
Oh! I am frightened.
I just saw a mouse!

• Read the children a version of "Jack and the Beanstalk".

Fill the gap

under	over	up	down	in	on

 The sky diver came _____ through the clouds.

 The girl got _____ the car.

 The boy went _____ to the top of the hill.

 The car went _____ the bridge.

 The cat sat _____ the chair.

 The boat went _____ the bridge.

Fill in the gaps to make the sentences.

The Pirate

The Pirate

By Jill Eggleton
Illustrations by Jim Storey

Teaching Points for Set 3 Book 7:   **sight words - down over under up**
letter recognition - bl sl
focus - positional language

The Pirate

Introducing the Story

Before reading the story ask the children to think about pirates:

What do you know about pirates?

What do pirates wear?

What did they do with the treasure they stole from other ships?

The Oral Story-Telling

Peg-leg Pete was a wicked pirate chief. He made the sailors row to the island.

"Ha,ha. I'll soon have my treasure," he said. He went up the hill and into the cave. "Ha, ha. Here is my treasure box and it's full of gold," he said. Peg-leg Pete carried the treasure down the hill and over the sand.

"Look, my hearties. I have gold, gold, gold!" he said. "Open up my treasure box."

The pirates opened the box. Inside there was no gold, no diamonds only rocks, rocks, rocks.

"GRRRRRRRR" said all the pirates.

Reading the Text

See Introduction: Reading the Text, p.8.

Talking about the Story

Ask the children:

Where did Peg-leg Pete find the treasure box?

What did you think was going to be in the treasure box?

What do you think happened to all the treasure?

Follow-up Activities

• Make a pirate hat.

Make a template of a pirate's hat as shown in the illustration below.

Let each child cut out two card outlines.

Tell the children to decorate one of these. They might like to try to copy the one from the book.

When they have done this help them to staple the two sides together.

Finally fit the hat on to the child's head and staple the bottom edges together so that the hat fits.

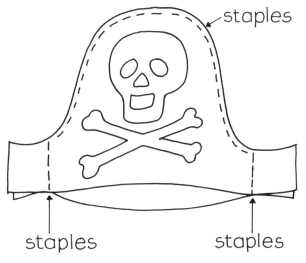

staples

staples   staples

• Find the Treasure.

Fill a sand tray with sand.

Ask the children to cut some straws into 3 cms lengths.

Cut one straw to make it approximately 6 cms long. This straw represents the place where the treasure is hidden.

Let the children place all the straws into the sand so that they all appear the same length.

The children can then ask their friends to guess which is the pirate treasure spot and let them select a straw.

• Read to the class the story, "Pirates" by C. Hawkins (Picture Lions).

The Animal Party

Introducing the Story

Before reading the story show the children the illustrations and invite them to comment upon the pictures and tell the story in their own way.

Reading the Text

See Introduction: Reading the Text, p.8.

Talking about the Story

Ask the children:

What did the lion eat and what did he do?

What did the monkey eat and what did he do?

What did the snake eat and what did he do?

What did the giraffe eat and what did he do?

What did the elephant eat and what happened?

Follow-up Activities

• Make a simple joke board for the children to read.

1 What time is it when an elephant sits on the table?
Time to get a new table!

2 What do you get if you cross a giraffe with a hedgehog?
An eleven metre hair brush.

3 Why do elephants have trunks?
They'd look silly with suitcases wouldn't they.

4 Why does a giraffe have a long neck?
To join his head to his shoulders.

Can anyone add to the list? Children can ask friends in other classes, brothers and sisters, or adults at home or at school.

• Game: "How strong is your table?"

Let each child make a table from duplo bricks and a thin sheet of card.

Let the children collect six small items to see if the table is strong enough to support them, e.g. tiddlywinks, lego brick, dice, pencil, scissors, toy car.

• Game: "Crash!"

Using bricks, blocks or rods let two or three children take it in turn to build a column with one brick on top of the other. The person who causes the column to fall down is the loser.

• Follow the instructions.

Make small flash cards of the words 'on', 'beside', 'over', 'under.'

Using the same six items collected for the above activity ask the children to perform an action but hold up the card for the position the item must take, e.g. Put the tiddlywink **on** the lego brick.

Put the pencil **beside** the scissors.

Put the tiddlywink **under** the dice.

Put the car **over** the tiddlywink, etc.

The Goat

Introducing the Story

Before reading the story ask the children:

What would you like to eat? e.g. a banana or a book. After the children have given their answer say, "But a goat likes both."

Would a cat like fish or plums?

Would a dog like meat or grass?

Would a mouse like pot plants or cheese?

Would a rabbit like dandelions or a tablecloth?

Would a bird like seeds or cabbages.

After every choice say, "But a goat likes both."

Reading the Text

See Introduction: Reading the Text, p.8.

Talking about the Story

Ask the children:

Can you remember what the goat ate?

What did Dad say to the goat?

What did Mum say to the goat?

Why couldn't the goat get under the fence?

Follow-up Activities

• Choose a page from the story, "The Goat" and read it to the child. Then shut the book and ask, "What page was I reading?" See if the child can search through the story and find the page you selected.

• Letter recognition. 'bl' and 'sl'

Give the children a copy of the photocopy master 27 (Activity Book B4).

Tell them they can look in any books or at words written on the wall.

Can they climb the ladders by finding words with these blends? They should put a word on each rung of the right ladder until they have written six words on each. The blends can come anywhere in the word e.g. ta**bl**e **sl**ide **bl**ue.

• Say the rhyme:

*Our goat ate up the flowers.
It ate up Dad's new shoe.
Our goat ate Mum's old hairbrush
And it ate my school book too!*

*Our goat ate the dog's biscuit.
It ate my pot of glue.
Our goat ate the cat's dinner
And it ate the bowl too!*

*I often stop to wonder
As our goat takes a drink.
What's happening in his tummy?
I really cannot think!*

• Say the following rhyme:

*Gus the goat's a greedy goat.
He crams everything down his throat.
He tried eating Mum's new coat.
Gus the greedy goat.*

*Gus the goat's a greedy goat.
He crams everything down his throat.
He tried to eat my sailing boat.
Gus the greedy goat.*

*Gus the goat's a greedy goat.
He crams everything down his throat.
He tried eating the milkman's note.
Gus, the greedy goat.*

• Read the class some of the Helen Piers Animal Stories (Methuen).

• Read the class a version of the story, "The Three Billy Goats Gruff".

Name_____

_____

Climb the ladder

sl   bl

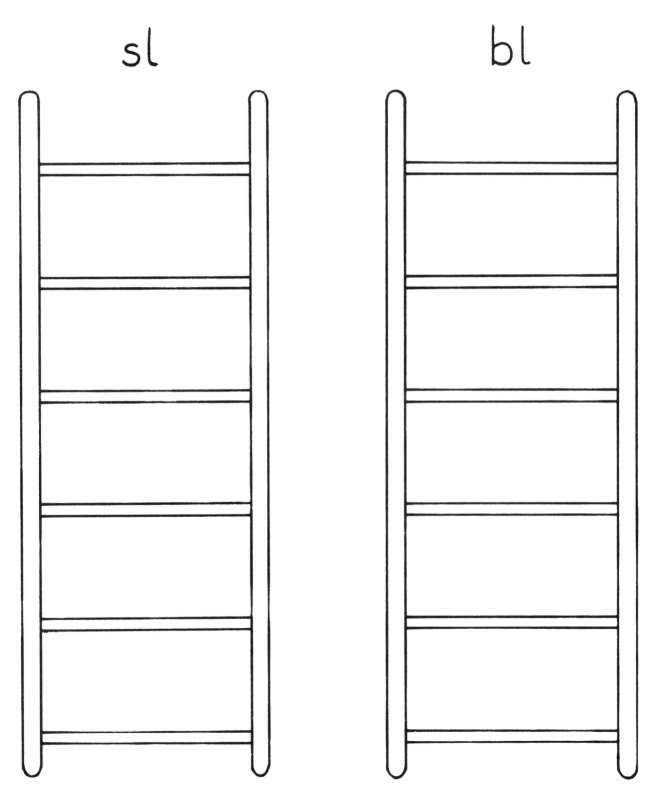

Find words with sl and bl in them.

Write the words you find on the correct ladder starting from the bottom rung

The Magic Machine

The Magic Machine

By Joy Cowley
Illustrations by Susan Moxley

Teaching Points for Set 3 Book 8:	sight words - in on put they letter recognition - pl focus - colours

The Magic Machine

Introducing the Story

Before reading the story ask the children:

Have you ever seen a rainbow?

What colours do you think are in a rainbow?

What is your favourite colour?

The Oral Story-Telling

Once upon a time the man who made the rain and the woman who made the sun met and decided to use their magic machine. First the sun woman put some orange colour into the magic machine. Then the rain man put some blue colour into the magic machine. The sun lady put in some yellow colour and the rain man put in some red colour. They both put in some violet colour and then they turned on the magic machine. What do you think came out? It was a beautiful rainbow.

Reading the Text

See Introduction: Reading the Text, p.8.

Talking about the Story

Ask the children:

Can you remember what colours the rain man and the sun woman put into the machine?

Do you think a rainbow comes from a magic machine?

What do we really need to make a rainbow? (sun and rain)

What are all the colours in the rainbow?

(red, orange, yellow, green, blue, indigo, violet)

Do you know any stories about rainbows?

Follow-up Activities

• Make a rainbow picture.

Using very watery paint ask the children to make a thick line of red paint across the top of their piece of paper.

Underneath add a line of watery orange paint. Continue until each rainbow colour has been added. There will be some colour running between each line and this will add to the rainbow effect. Allow the paintings to dry and then make a giant rainbow for the classroom wall by putting the painted papers into a large arc across the wall, overlapping at the bottom to form a curve.

• Make a rainbow spinning wheel.

Cut out two circles of card.

Draw rings on each circle to represent the colours of the rainbow.

Glue the two circles together.

Make two holes in the circles on either side of the centre.

Thread a piece of string through the holes and tie the ends of the string together to make a continuous loop with the colour circle in the middle. Holding one hand still, wind up the string and colour circle with the other.

When it is wound tight pull the string taut on either side of the circle.

Using this action of pulling both hands apart, and then letting them draw together through the action of the spinning card, the circle should spin quickly.

Ask the children to guess which colour they will see when the disc is spinning.

• Sing the song: "Sing a Rainbow".

Red and yellow and purple and green,
Orange and violet and blue.
I can sing a rainbow, sing a rainbow,
Sing a rainbow too.

• Show the children the book, "Colour Dance" by Ann Jonas (Walker).

• Show the children Ladybird "Colour" Book.

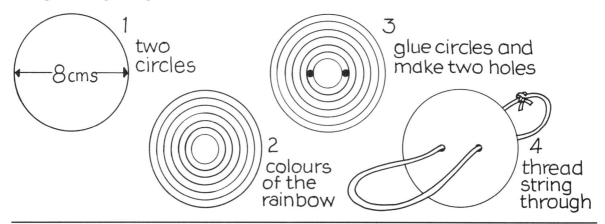

1 two circles — 8cms

2 colours of the rainbow

3 glue circles and make two holes

4 thread string through

Go to Sleep!

Introducing the Story

Before reading the story ask the children:

What time do you go to bed?

Do you sleep in a single bed or in a bunk bed?

Do you like taking a cuddly toy to bed with you?

Do you think of excuses so that you don't have to go to bed yet?

Do you always go straight to sleep?

Do you sometimes play after the light has been turned out?

Reading the Text

See Introduction: Reading the Text, p.8.

Talking about the Story

Some questions to ask:

Can you remember what the children played with? (computer, skateboard, ball, pillows)

Do you think that they really tricked Dad?

What might Dad have noticed that had been moved since he turned the light out?

Follow-up Activities

• Say the rhyme:

Dad puts us to bed
And turns out the light.
Then he shuts the door
And says Goodnight.

We jump out of bed.
We turn on the light.
We jump on the beds
And have a pillow fight.

Dad comes up the stairs
And looks round the door.
We have got our eyes shut.
Snore! Snore! Snore!

• Ask the children to share with you the reasons why they cannot get to sleep.

Do they wake up before Mum or Dad? What do they do?

• Look at the wordless picture book, "Moonlight" by Jan Ormerod (Picture Puffin).

• Read with the class, "Can't You Sleep, Little Bear?" by Martin Waddell (Walker Books).

• Read, " When Sheep Cannot Sleep" by Satoshi Kitamura (Beaver Books).

The Supermarket Baby

Introducing the Story

Before reading the story ask the children to look at the illustrations and ask the children to identify the various foods. This will help prepare them for the vocabulary in the story.

Reading the Text

As this story consolidates the vocabulary of the previous stories the children should, as far as possible, lead the reading.

Talking about the Story

Ask the children:

What was put in the trolley?

Who had a ride in the trolley?

What did the baby do?

Follow-up Activities

• Say these food riddles and ask the children to guess what you are describing:

I am brown or white. I am yellow in the middle. I come in a special box. What am I? (eggs)

I grow in the ground. I have lots of layers. You might cry if you chopped me up. What am I? (onions)

I am brown or white. I have a crust. You can put me in a toaster. What am I? (bread)

I am small and red. I am picked in the summer. You might eat me with cream. What am I? (strawberries)

• Give each child a copy of the photocopy master 28 (Activity Book B5). Tell the children that there are lots of things wrong in the picture. Can they spot them? See if they can put a circle around ten things that are wrong and then colour them in. Ask the children to write in the space provided which they think is the funniest. (The answers are: mirror image notice; child pushing mother in trolley; inverted pyramid of tins; ice cream upside down; teapot on lady's head; ball among the apples; man in ballet shoes; trouser legs different length; boy with one shoe, one boot; one large trolley wheel.)

• Make a bowl of fruit.

Mix equal amounts of flour and salt. Add a little water. Mix to a stiff dough. Shape into apples, pears, bananas, strawberries, etc.

Alternatively, roll 'pastry' flat to approximately half a centimetre thick. Cut out fruit shapes. Make a small hole near the top. Allow to dry on a radiator or window-sill overnight. Paint when dry. Either display the fruit in a fruit bowl, or hang up the fruit using string threaded through the small hole.

What is wrong?

I think _____

_____ is the funniest.

Colour all the things that are wrong. Which one is the funniest?

The Seals

The Seals

By Joy Cowley
Illustrations by Madeline Beasley

Teaching Points for Set 3 Book 9:

sight words - big little
letter recognition - sh
focus - size

The Seals

Introducing the Story

Before reading the story ask the children:

Have you ever seen seals at the zoo or on T.V.?

Have you ever seen seals in the sea?

What do you think seals eat?

What do you think eats seals?

The Oral Story-Telling

One day some little seals were playing around their parents. "Arf! Arf! We are hungry," they said. The big seals said, "We will chase some fish in the sea." Then they saw a dark shadow in the water. It was a shark. The shark had rows of very sharp teeth. It was looking for seals to eat. The big seals swam fast. The little seals swam fast too. The shark was getting closer and closer. It opened its huge mouth to catch the seals. The big seals jumped out of the water. But where are the little seals? Have they got away from the shark? "Arf! Arf!" they hear. The little seals are sitting safely on a rock.

Reading the Text

See Introduction: Reading the Text, p.8.

Talking about the Story

Ask the children:

Why did the seals go in the water?

What did the seals chase?

What chased the seals?

Did they all escape?

Follow-up Activities

• The shark has snapped the beginning off each word. See if you can add the 'sh' sound and make the words complete again, e.g. ..adow = shadow

..ape; ..eet; ..ine; ..oe; ..ut; ..ake; ..arp; ..elf; ..ip; ..op; ..ow; ..ampoo; ..eep; ..ell; ..irt; ..ort; ..out.

• Rhyme: "Six sleek seals".

Six sleek seals
Swimming in the sea.
Shark swims swiftly
And wants them for his tea.

Six sleek seals
Swim for the shore.
Shark swims swiftly
But the seals swim more.

Six sleek seals
Sunbathe in the sun.
Shark swims swiftly
But catches not a one.

• Discuss with children what the young of different animals are called. A baby seal is a pup. What else is called a pup, or puppy? What is a baby cat? Cow? Sheep? Horse?

• Read with the children, "First Facts: Sharks" by Kate Petty (Franklin Watts).

Oh No, Francisco!

Introducing the Story

Before reading the story ask the children:

Do you like painting?

Do you do painting at home?

What would happen if you put paint on the wall?

Reading the Text

See Introduction: Reading the Text, p.8.

Talking about the Story

Some questions to ask:

Where did Francisco put the paint? (wall, toys, mat, bed, himself)

What do you think his mother will do?

What would **your** mother do?

Follow-up Activities

• Being tidy.

Francisco was very messy. Are you sometimes messy? Do you put things away in the right place?

At home: Where should you put your books? Coat? Shoes? Toys?

At school: Where should you put your coat? Shoes? Books? Pencils? Paints? Scissors?

• Give each child a copy of the photocopy master 29. There are two identical drawings of four items but one is big and one is little. The child should write the words 'big' and 'little' over the dotted lines given, then write the correct word under the rest of the items.

• Make up poster paints in red, yellow, blue and green and pour one colour into each of four shallow trays. Each child can choose a colour for finger painting on to a large communal sheet of paper. Alternatively, the children can use sculpted potato halves, or halved peppers for printing.

• Read the children, "Mouse Paint" by Ellen Stoll Walsh (Orchard Books).

• Read the story, "Tom and Pippo Make a Mess" by Helen Oxenbury (Walker Books).

Vegetable prints

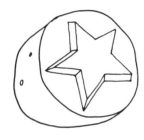

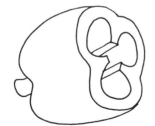
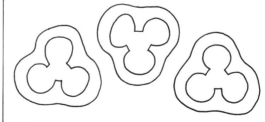

The Hole in the Ground

Introducing the Story

Before reading the story ask the children:

Have you ever seen any machines digging up the ground?

What did the machine look like?

Why was it digging a hole?

Why does the driver wear a hard hat?

Reading the Text

See Introduction: Reading the Text, p.8.

Talking about the Story

Questions to ask:

Why did the digger come to the school?

What kind of wheels has the digger got?

Would you like a swimming pool in your school playground?

Follow-up Activities

- In pairs ask the children to make a 'machine' from boxes, cardboard rolls, etc. Ask the children to describe what their machine can do.

- Talk about animals that make holes and live in them (moles, badgers, foxes, rabbits).

- Collect machines.

  Ask the children to think of as many machines as they can and put them on a chart under headings:

  What machines help us at home? (vacuum cleaner, washing machine, iron, fridge, blender, toaster, freezer)

  What machines help us at school? (computer, photocopier, tape recorder, clock, calculator)

What machines help on a farm? (tractor, hayturner, combine harvester, grass cutter, milking equipment)

What machines do we see in the street? (excavator, bicycle, car, truck, road drill, concrete mixer)

- Say the following rhyme and ask the children to act it out.

  Say each verse a little louder than the one before.

  There was one person digging
  A hole in the ground.
  He made a little hole
  And he made a little mound.
  But along came the digger
  And made it bigger.

  There were two people digging
  A hole in the ground.
  They made a big hole
  And they made a big mound.
  But along came the digger
  And made it bigger.

  There were three people digging
  A hole in the ground.
  They made the hole enormous
  And they made an enormous mound.
  But along came the digger
  And made it bigger!

- Read the book "Monster Machines" by Paul Strickland (Wayland).

- Read with the class, "Car – See How it Works" by Angela Royston (Frances Lincoln).

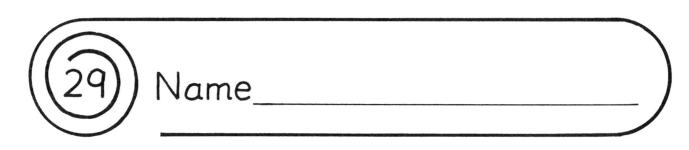

29 Name_____

_____

Which is big and which is little?

big

little

Write the word big or little under the drawing.

The Hungry Lion

The Hungry Lion
By Jillian Cutting
Illustrations by Jan van der Voo

Teaching Points for Set 3 Book 10:	sight words - and my too
	letter recognition - sp
	focus - ordinals - first, second, third

The Hungry Lion

Introducing the Story

Before reading the story ask the children:

Where do you think a lion lives?

What do you think a lion eats?

What will the zebra, deer and elephant do if they see a lion coming?

The Oral Story-Telling

One day lion was very hungry. What can I eat? he said. He saw the elephant and he thought, "I will eat elephant." But elephant said, "You cannot eat me. I am too big." Next, lion saw monkey and he thought, "I will eat monkey." But monkey said, "You cannot eat me. I am too clever." Next, lion saw crocodile and he thought, "I will eat crocodile." But crocodile said, "You cannot eat me. I am too fierce." Then lion saw zebra and he thought, "I will eat zebra." But zebra said, " You cannot eat me. I am too fast." So lion sneaked up on all the animals when they were not looking. "I **will** eat someone," he said. Just then elephant heard lion and zebra smelled lion. "Run!" said the animals, "Lion is hungry." And all the animals ran away. So lion went hungry that day.

Reading the Text

See Introduction: Reading the Text, p.8.

Talking about the Story

Ask the children:

Can you remember why elephant said lion should not eat him? (He was too big.)

(Monkey said "Too clever"; crocodile, "Too fierce"; zebra, "Too fast".)

Follow-up Activities

• Tell the children the Aesop's Fable about the wise jackal.

• Say the rhyme:

Walking through the jungle,
What did I see?
A big lion roaring,
At me, me, me!

Walking through the jungle,
What did I see?
An elephant trumpeting,
At me, me, me!

Walking through the jungle,
What did I see?
A baby monkey laughing,
At me, me, me!

Walking through the jungle,
What did I see?
A crocodile snapping,
At me, me, me!

Walking through the jungle,
What did I see?
A zebra stampeding,
At me, me, me!

• Make a number of cards with the word 'and' on them. Say the following phrases and ask two or more children to race each other to pick up an 'and' card when they hear it said. (Bread **and** butter; fish **and** chips; cup **and** saucer; knife **and** fork; strawberries **and** cream.) Count who has the most cards.

127

- Say the verse getting faster and faster like a steam train leaving the station:

  Coffee, coffee; (slowly)

  Cheese and biscuits, cheese and biscuits; (a little quicker, with the rhythm of wheels on a track)

  Plums and custard, plums and custard; (faster)

  Fish and chips, fish and chips; (very fast)

  Soooooooup!

- Read the story, "My Brown Bear Barney" by Dorothy Butler (Picture Knight).

- Read to the children the story, "The Lion in the Meadow" by Margaret Mahy (Picture Lions).

The Pet Show

Introducing the Story

Before reading the story ask the children:

  What do you think happens at a pet show?

  If you went to a pet show what pet would you take?

  If you were a pet show judge what would you ask each animal to do? (dog, monkey, frog, spider)

Reading the Text

See Introduction: Reading the Text, p.8.

Talking about the Story

Ask the children:

  Can you remember who got first prize? (spider)

  Who got second prize? (dog)

  Who got third prize? (goldfish)

  Which pet would you give first prize to?

Follow-up Activities

- Say the following rhyme:

  I went to the pet show.
  My dad said, "It's not wise."
  I took along my pet toad
  *And I got **third** prize.*

  I went to the pet show
  My dad said, "It's not wise."
  I took along my pet snake
  *And I got **second** prize.*

  I went to the pet show
  My dad said, "It's not wise."
  I took along my pet slug
  *And I got **first** prize.*

- Talk about how different creatures have different numbers of legs. Compare, e.g. a spider, bee, cow, person, millipede, earthworm…Ask the children to draw an animal with eight legs; with six legs; with four legs; with two legs; with no legs. They could be real or made up.

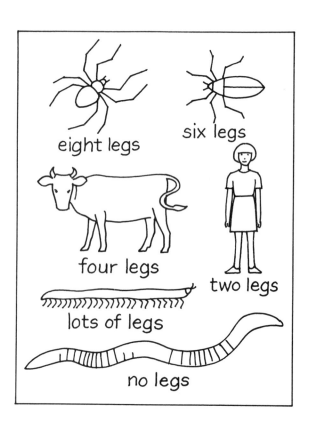

eight legs

six legs

four legs

two legs

lots of legs

no legs

- Talk about first/second/third and explain the relationship between numerals (one, two, three) and ordinals (first, second, third).
- Give the children a box of counters. Ask them, "Do you remember the spider from the story ? What could it do? (crawl and spin webs). What do you notice about **sp**ider and **sp**in? Listen to these words and put down a counter every time you hear a word beginning with 'sp'. Include in the list the following words: space, spade, spaghetti, spanner, spare, spark, sparkle, sparrow, speak, spear, special, speech, speed, spell, spend, spice, spike, spill, spin, spinach, splash, split, spoon, sport, spring.

The Computer Story

Introducing the Story

Before reading the story ask the children:

Have you ever used a computer?

What sort of things are on each computer key?

Have you tried to type your name?

Reading the Text

See Introduction: Reading the Text, p.8.

Talking about the Story

- Ask the children to look at the story and look at the pictures on the computer screen.

Can you say which letters are missing on each page?

Follow-up Activities

- Give each child a copy of the photocopy master 30 (Activity Book B6).

Ask the children to draw a picture of themselves, their pets, their family, etc. They can then colour the pictures in.

- Children should work in pairs to reproduce on to the classroom computer the text from the story. They could print out the text and read it to one another.
- Sing the alphabet together. See the alphabet rhymes on p.88 (Set 2 Book 10).
- Make a computer keyboard.

Look at a computer keyboard. Count the number of letters across the top line of the alphabet. There are ten. Draw ten circles in a line using a coin. Then draw nine circles in the middle line and seven circles in the last line. Now look at each capital letter on the keyboard and try to write its small letter in the correct circle.

Name_____

_____

All about me

I am a

I am a

This is my

This is my

This is my

_____ _____ _____

This is my

_____ _____ _____

Write the words and draw pictures in the boxes about yourself and your family.

Sharks

Teaching Points for Set 4 Book 1:	sight words - fast looked
	letter recognition - st
	focus - sentences

Sharks

Introducing the Text

Before reading the text ask the children:

Where do sharks live?

What do they eat?

Do you know the names of any different kinds of sharks?

How big do you think they are?

Setting the Scene

As this is a non-fiction text it is necessary to try to get children to understand some of the differences between fiction and non-fiction and therefore an oral telling is less applicable. With this text spend time talking to the children about the use of photographs and how the cover of the book gives us a good idea that this book could contain either a true story or it could be a book about sharks and how they live, what they look like and what they eat.

If possible, support this text with other non-fiction texts and show the children other photographs. It could be an opportunity to talk about protected species and the fact that even though sharks have a bad reputation this is no reason to exterminate them. Children are likely to have an impression that all sharks are enormous and dangerous and this again could be addressed.

Shark facts:

They are found in all oceans except the Antarctic.

They have very few enemies apart from other sharks.

The largest shark is called the whale shark. It is harmless to humans.

The smallest shark is only 15 cms long.

If a shark looses a tooth another will grow.

Sharks have very good eyesight and an excellent sense of smell.

Sharks keep the seas clean. They eat up dying and infirm fish.

Reading the Text

See Introduction: Reading the Text, p.8.

Talking about the Text

Ask the children:

Can you remember the names of any sharks?

What do sharks like to eat?

What do you know about sharks' teeth?

Follow-up Activities

- Show the class other books about sharks e.g. "First facts: Sharks" (Franklin Watts).

  "Let's look it up: Sharks:" (Franklin Watts).

  "Let's look at sharks" (Wayland).

  "Picture Library: Sharks" (Franklin Watts).

- Make a collage of fish shapes in the sea.

  Draw a big shark chasing all the little fish.

- Game: "Flap the Shark".

  Make some large fish shapes about 20 cms long from newspaper.

  Make the same numbers of shark shape flappers from card. They need to be a little larger than the fish.

Play chase the fish by flapping with the shark across the hall floor.

The first child to flap the fish across the hall wins.

The Skier

Introducing the Story

Before reading the story ask the children:

What do skiers wear?

Where do people go to ski?

Do skiers go fast or slowly down the mountains?

Why do skiers sometimes fall over?

Reading the Text

See Introduction: Reading the Text, p.8.

Talking about the Story

Ask the children:

Can you remember how the skier got up the mountain?

Can you remember how the skier got down the mountain?

What happened to the skier?

Why do you think she was wearing a helmet?

Follow-up Activities

• Riddle: "What am I doing?"

I wear clothes to keep me warm.
I like deep snow.
I wear a helmet.
I can go down mountains very fast.
I am.....

I wear short trousers.
I shoot at a goal.
I can kick or head the ball.
The ball is black and white.
I am playing.....

I am in the kitchen.
I stand by the cooker.
I look in the oven.
I stir the gravy.
I am.....

I sit on a seat.
I hold a wheel.
I look at the road.
I poop the horn.
I am.....

• Letter recognition: 'st'.

Give each child a copy of the photocopy master 31.

Ask the children to look very carefully at the picture and to draw a circle round any picture that they can see that starts with 'st'. See if they can find ten. (stile, steeple, stable, stream, stem or stalk, stick, stones, stirrup, straw, storm cloud)

• Make a plan of a ski run.

Ask the group to tell you where to put things on the plan.

Provide a large sheet of paper and ask the children:

Where should the race start? (at the top of the mountain)

What should we draw to show the start of the race? (small hut)

Does the race course go straight down or curve? (Draw a curvy course)

How does the skier know where to go? (The red and blue flags mark the course.)

Where would the race finish? (at the bottom of the mountain)

What should we draw to show the end of the race? (a 'Finish' banner)

Where should the crowds stand? (behind the barrier)

Are there any trees on the mountainside? (Yes, there are fir trees.)

Let the children draw and cut out different skiers and place them on the mountain.

The Cycle Race

Introducing the Story

Before reading the story ask the children:

Have you ever seen a cycle race?

What do the cyclists wear?

Which parts of their bodies do you think get very tired?

Do the cyclists go very fast? What makes you think this?

Do the cyclists have special racing bicycles?

Reading the Text

See Introduction: Reading the Text, p.8.

Talking about the Story

Ask the children:

What did the cyclists have to put on before they could go in the race?

What did the man wave to start the race?

Would you like to race on your bicycle?

How do you know that the winner was pleased?

Follow-up Activities

• Talk to the children about the different wheels that they know:

How many wheels has a wheelbarrow?

How many wheels has a racing bike?

What vehicles have lots of wheels?

Are wheels all the same size?

Are the wheels on a racing bike different from other bikes?

See p.60 (Set 2 Book 3) for instructions on how to make a bar chart showing vehicles with different numbers of wheels.

• Say the rhyme:

I am in a cycle race,
I go very fast.
If I cycle harder
No-one will go past.

I am in a running race,
I go very fast.
If I run much harder
No-one will go past.

I am in a skiing race,
I go very fast.
If I try much harder
No-one will go past.

I am in a rowing race
I do not go fast.
Where is everybody?
Oh dear - I am the last.

• Make a collage showing different wheels. Cut out as many pictures of wheels as possible and stick them on to a sheet of sugar paper.

• Look at the book "Readabout: Wheels" (Franklin Watts).

• Sing the song: "The wheels of the bike go round and round." See p.159 (Set 4 Book 8).

The bell on the bike goes ring ring ring.
The chain on the bike goes rattle rattle rattle.

Start with st

Draw a circle around the pictures of words starting with st.
See if you can find ten.

Dr Sprocket Makes a Rocket

Dr Sprocket Makes a Rocket
By Joy Cowley
Illustrations by Philip Webb

Teaching Points for Set 4 Book 2:	sight words - from makes letter recognition - bl focus - rhyme

Dr Sprocket Makes a Rocket

Introducing the Story

Before reading the story ask the children:

Have you ever seen a rocket launch on T.V.?

Where do you think the rockets are going?

Would you like to ride in a rocket?

The Oral Story-Telling

Dr Sprocket has a plan. She wants to make a rocket. First she collects wooden boxes and she separates each panel of wood to make the frame of the rocket. She collects old cans. She hammers them flat and makes them into the metal casing of the rocket. She makes her rocket out of some computers and some old pans. She makes it from old chairs and old wires. She makes it from old clocks and old tyres. She makes it from old buckets. Near the front of the rocket is a big red starting button. Dr Sprocket pushes the starting button with a broom. "This should start the engine," thinks Dr Sprocket. Do you think Dr Sprocket's rocket will fly?

Reading the Text

See Introduction: Reading the Text, p.8.

Talking about the Story

Ask the children:

Can you remember what Dr Sprocket made her rocket from? (boxes, cans, computers, pans, chairs, wires, clocks, tyres, buckets)

What did she use to start the rocket?

Did it fly off?

Where do you think she will go?

Follow-up Activities

- Join in the rhyme:

  Dr Sprocket makes a rocket.
  She makes it from old boxes.
  She makes it from old cans.
  She makes it from computers.
  She makes it from .....

  (Continue reading the story, omitting the rhyming word for children to supply.)

- Give each child a copy of the photocopy master 32 (Activity Book B7). After practising writing the words 'makes it from', they should write and colour the 'Zoo-oo-oom'.

- Say the rhyme:

  I want to build a rocket
  To travel to the moon.
  I've got some things to make it.
  I've got scissors and a spoon.

  I want to build a rocket
  To travel through the sky.
  I've got some things to make it.
  I've got a pencil and a pie.

I want to build a rocket
To travel far away.
I've got some things to make it.
I've got hankies and some hay.

I tried to build my rocket.
I used all the things I've said.
But my rocket was quite useless
So I'll stay on earth instead.

• Build a class rocket from shoe and eggboxes. Paint and decorate it.

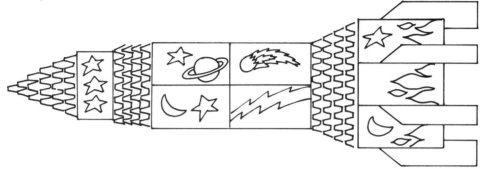

The Greedy Gobbler

Introducing the Story

Before reading the story ask the children:

Do you know what a vacuum cleaner is?

Do you call it a hoover?

Who does the hoovering in your house?

What does a vacuum cleaner suck up?

What do you think a greedy gobbler vacuum cleaner might suck up?

Reading the Text

See Introduction: Reading the Text, p.8.

Talking about the Story

Ask the children:

Can you remember all the things the greedy gobbler gobbled? (dust, mat, chair, cat, cups, plates, ball, skates)

What happened to it in the end?

Follow-up Activities

• Ask the children to fill in the missing rhyming words:

It gobbled up the dust.

It gobbled up the mat.

It gobbled up the chair.

It gobbled up the .....

(Continue reading the story in this way omitting the rhyming word for the children to supply.)

• Things about the home.

What do you call the machine for washing clothes? Drying clothes? Mowing the grass? Keeping food cool? Keeping food frozen? Cooking food? Boiling water?

• Guess what appliances these funny names might refer to?

Greedy gobbler (vacuum cleaner), sloshy spinner (washing machine), rumble tumbler (tumble dryer), grass gobbler (lawn mower), cooly chiller (fridge), icy chiller (freezer), hotty baker (cooker), spouty boiler (kettle).

• Read to the children the story, "The Cat in the Hat" by Dr Seuss (Collins).

• Read "Doing the Washing" by Sarah Garland (Picture Puffin).

The Wind

Introducing the Story

Before reading the story ask the children:

Have you ever been outside on a windy day?

Can you see the wind?

How can you tell if it is a windy day?

What toys are best when it is windy? (kite, windmill)

Reading the Text

See Introduction: Reading the Text, p.8.

Talking about the Story

Ask the children:

Who gave the girl the balloon?

Where did the balloon go? (over the lake, over the trees, over the cars, over the house)

Where did the balloon land?

Who had it as a birthday present?

Follow-up Activities

• Make a windmill.

1 Use a square piece of paper. Fold the paper corner to corner both ways to give diagonal creases, and end to end both ways to give horizontal and vertical creases.

2 Cut from each corner along the diagonal crease towards the centre.

3 Fold one section of each 'cut diagonal' in towards the centre leaving the other four 'cut diagonals' to be the outer sails of the windmill. Fix the folds at the centre with a split pin or sellotape.

• Play the 'bl' game:

Ask the children if they can guess the 'bl' word that you are thinking of. Give simple definitions of the following 'bl' words:

black, blue, blink, blackberry, blackbird, blackboard, blanket, blood, blind, blister, blouse, bluebell, blunt.

• Say the rhyme:

Who knows where the wind goes?
Nobody knows.
First it blows and blows and blows
And then it goes.

Who knows what the wind sees?
Nobody knows.
It blows the leaves down from the trees
And then it goes.

Who knows what the wind hears?
Nobody knows.
It hears the roar of the sea on the shore
And then it goes.

• Read the Aesop's Fable, "The Sun and the Wind".

• Read the poem, "Wind on the Hill" from "Now We Are Six" by A. A. Milne (Mammoth).

• Read "The Wind Blew" by Pat Hutchins (Picture Puffin).

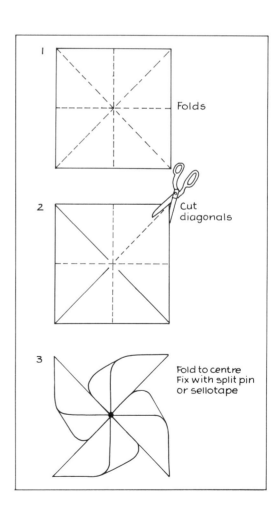

1 Folds

2 Cut diagonals

3 Fold to centre
Fix with split pin
or sellotape

Write the words

	makes	it	from

She _____ __ _____

She _____ __ _____

She _____ __ _____

She _____ __ _____

Dr Sprocket flies her rocket

Z oo-oo-oom

At the Fair

By Jillian Cutting
Illustrations by Tracey Maroney

| Teaching Points for Set 4 Book 3: | sight words - of took
letter recognition - sw
focus - swimming |

At the Fair

Introducing the Story

Before reading the story ask the children:

Have you ever been to a fun-fair or a theme park?

Which ride did you like best?

Was there any ride you did not want to go on?

Have you any photos of your visit?

Have you got a favourite photograph of yourself?

The Oral Story-Telling

My dad had a new camera and he loved taking photographs. One day all of my family went to the fair. Dad took a photograph of me on the roller coaster. Dad took a photograph of Mum on the ferris wheel. He took a photograph of Grandad on the merry-go-round. He took a photograph of my sister on the ghost train. He took a photograph of Grandma on the log ride. Then Dad took a photograph of everyone. We couldn't wait to see the photographs of our great day out.

Reading the Text

See Introduction: Reading the Text, p.8.

Talking about the Story

Ask the children:

What did Dad like doing?

How many rides can you remember? (roller coaster, ferris wheel, merry-go-round, ghost train, log ride)

Which ride would you have liked best?

Follow-up Activities

• Give each child a copy of the photocopy master 33 (Activity Book B8) and ask, "What did Dad photograph?"

The children must write in the missing words, increasing the number of words to be written with each line. Labelled pictures help with the animals.

Make sure the children start each letter at the correct place.

• Say the rhyme:

Dad took a photograph.
What do you think he took?
It was me in a fancy dress
Dressed up as a cook.

Dad took a photograph.
It took us by surprise.
It was me at the school sports
Winning the first prize.

Dad finished off the film
With all the snaps of me.
But when he opened the camera back
Oh dear! What did he see?

The camera was quite empty
Oh no! I could have cried.
There would be no photos
'Cos there was no film inside!

• Ask other members of staff to let you have a photograph of themselves with their pets. Put these together in a big book. Write underneath each photograph "This is .... with her pet ....."

At the Swimming Pool

Introducing the Story

Before reading the story ask the children:

Who do you go swimming with?

Where do you go?

What do you like playing in the water?

Do you wear armbands or do you swim by yourself?

Reading the Text

See Introduction: Reading the Text, p.8.

Talking about the Story

Ask the children:

What did the notice say at the poolside?

Why do you think the man did not want the children to dive in?

Why do you think the man did not want the children to jump in?

Why has the man got a whistle around his neck?

Follow-up Activities

• Ask the children what they think the rules at a swimming pool should be?

Would they allow people to run around the pool edge?

Would they stop people jumping? Pushing? Diving?

Would they stop people shouting?

Help the children to make a poster to display their rules.

• Game: "Take-a-step".

Tell the children that they can only take a step forward from a base line toward you if they can hear and tell you a 'sw' word. Stand a distance away from them. Say a range of words for the children to listen for including some of the 'sw' words listed below. The first child to say the word takes a step forward. Before they can take the last step they must say which letters make the sound 'sw'.

Some 'sw' words: swim, space, steam, scrap, sweep, swap, straw, sweater, story, slug, sweet, swan, swift, slice, switch, stairs, stamp, swing.

• Read to the class, "My Visit to the Swimming Pool" by Diana Bentley (Wayland).

• Share with the children, "Topsy and Tim Go Swimming" by Jean and Gareth Adamson (Blackie).

Swimming Rules

Wash your feet

No running

No pushing

No diving at shallow end

Leave your towel in the changing room

The Big Dive

Introducing the Story

Before reading the story ask the children:

Can anyone in your family dive?

Do they dive from the poolside or a diving board?

Have you seen any diving on T.V.?

Reading the Text

See Introduction: Reading the Text, p.8.

Talking about the Story

Some questions to ask:

Do you like to dive from a diving board?

Do you like to jump from a diving board? Where do you do it?

Do you think the girl in the story was clever to do such a thing?

Follow-up Activities

• Play: "Be brave".

Make a set of 20 small cards with two or three letter words taken from the sight vocabulary list. Put a pile of counters on the table. Each child takes it in turn to pick up a card. If the child reads the word correctly he or she can take one counter. If the children are 'brave' they can try to write the word, without copying. If they do so correctly they can have a counter for each letter in the word. The winner is the child with the most counters.

• Pre-diving warm-up exercises.

Say to the children and get them to follow the actions:

Up I stretch on tippy toe,
Down to touch my heels I go.
Up again my arms I send,
Down again my knees I bend.

• Game: "Chinese whispers".

Send the following secret messages around a circle of children, "Do you like to swim or swing?" "Would you like to swap a sweet?" "Let's switch sweaters."

• Say the rhyme about diving and encourage the children to participate with actions:

I'm swimming in the swimming pool.
Swimming to and fro. (Swimming actions.)
I think I'll dive into the pool. (Mime diving action.)
I think I'll have a go.

I'm climbing up and up the steps, (Mime climbing.)
Until I reach the top.
I walk to the edge of the diving board (Mime walking.)
And then I suddenly stop. (Stop suddenly.)

I look down into the pool. (Peer over edge.)
It looks so far away. (Mime looking a long way down.)
Perhaps I won't dive after all, (Shake head.)
Or I'll do it another day.

I climb down and down the steps. (Mime climbing down.)
I wish I'd tried to dive.
I'll definitely do it some day, (Punch clenched fist into palm of other hand.)
But now I'm only five! (Hold up five fingers.)

• Look together at "My Sport: Swimming" (Franklin Watts).

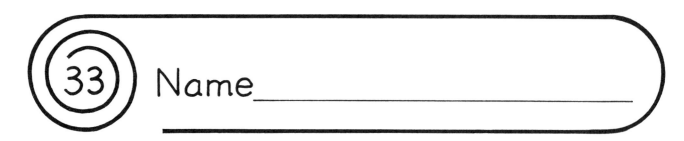

33 Name_____
_____

What did Dad photograph?

Dad took a photograph of a cat

Dad took a photograph _ _ dog

Dad ____ _ photograph _ _ bird

____ ____ _ photograph _ _ fish

____ ____ _ photograph _ _ cow

cat   dog   bird   fish   cow

Fill in the missing words. Colour the pictures.

The Blueberry Pie

Teaching Points for Set 4 Book 4:	sight words - did not letter recognition - ch focus - ordinals

The Blueberry Pie

Introducing the Story

Before reading the story ask the children:

What do you like best to eat?

What do you like best in a pie?

What kind of berries go into a pie? (blackberries, gooseberries, blackcurrants, redcurrants)

Have you ever heard of blueberries?

Why do you think they are called blueberries?

The Oral Story-Telling

Mary baked the nicest blueberry pie in town. Everyone came to her cafe to have some of her blueberry pie. One day Mary went to cut a slice of pie, but the pie had gone. "Who stole the blueberry pie?" asked Mary. "Not I," said the first cook. "I did not steal the blueberry pie." "Not I," said the second cook. "Not I," said the third cook. "Not I," said the fourth cook. Mary had a good idea. She knew that when you eat blueberries your tongue goes blue. So can you guess what she did? She made all the cooks stick out their tongues. But no one had a blue tongue. So she never knew who stole that pie. So she made lots more pies.

Reading the Text

See Introduction: Reading the Text, p.8.

Talking about the Story

Ask the children:

Who had stolen the blueberry pie?

How do you know?

Do you think the little dog might steal another one?

What do you think might happen?

Follow-up Activities

• Question time: "Did you like?"

Ask the children to reply either, "I did" or "I did not" to the following questions :

When you were a baby did you like sitting in your pram? Eating slugs? Making mud pies? Having your hair washed? Sitting in your push-chair?

• Give each child a copy of the photocopy master 34 (Activity Book B9). They will need to copy the name of the right child, to answer the questions of who is first, second, third and fourth. When they have finished, they may colour the picture.

• Say the nursery rhyme:

Little Jack Horner sat in the corner,
Eating a Christmas pie.
He put in his thumb,
And pulled out a plum,
And said, "What a good boy am I."

• Read with the children, "Wait and See" by Tony Bradman and Eileen Browne (Methuen).

• Read to the children the story, "The Little Red Hen" (Ladybird).

In the Night

Introducing the Story

Before reading the story ask the children:

Do you have something to eat just before you go to bed?

Do you ever feel hungry in the night?

What do you think your mum or dad would say if you sneaked some food from the fridge in the night?

Reading the Text

See Introduction: Reading the Text, p.8.

Talking about the Story

Ask the children:

What did Dad, Grandma, Sister and Brother do in the night?

Why did they not want any breakfast?

What do you think Mum said when she knew what had happened in the night?

Follow-up Activities

• Say the chant:

Dad felt empty in the night,
So he crept out of his bed.
He went into the kitchen.
He opened the fridge and said,
"I'm hungry!"

Grandma felt empty in the night,
So she crept out of her bed.
She went into the kitchen.
She opened the fridge and said,
"I'm hungry!"

Sister woke up in the night,
So she crept out of her bed.
She went into the kitchen.
She opened the fridge and said,
"I'm hungry!"

Brother felt hungry in the night,
So he crept out of his bed.
He went into the kitchen.
He opened the fridge and said,
"I'm hungry!"

Mum woke up in the morning.
"I must get everyone fed."
She called the family to breakfast
But, "We're not hungry," they said.

• Say the rhyme and play the game:

Isn't it funny that a bear likes honey?
Buzz, buzz, I wonder why he does!
Go to sleep, Mr Bear.
Wake up, Mr Bear.

Children sit in a circle with one child pretending to be a bear, sitting in the middle of the circle. With the first three lines of the rhyme, the child pretends to eat some honey and then goes to sleep.

The teacher indicates a particular child who stands up quietly. The other children call out, "Wake up, Mr Bear!"

The child in the middle of the circle now tries to run round outside the circle after the child who has stood up. This child must try to run round the outside of the circle and get back to his or her place in the circle before "Mr Bear" catches up.

• Listen to the sound.

Ask the children, "Can you hear the 'ch' sound in kitchen?" Ask them to put down a counter every time they hear the 'ch' sound, and say whether it is at the beginning, the middle, or the end.

Some 'ch' sounds: branch, brooch, church, bunch, bachelor, beech, butcher, approach, attach, catch, chain, chalk, chance, change, chapter, charge, hatch, match, fetch, clutch, crouch.

• Read with the class, "The Very Hungry Caterpillar" by Eric Carle (Picture Puffin).

Number 30 Rap Street

Introducing the Story

Before reading the story ask the children:

What musical instruments do you know?

Do people play musical instruments in houses near you?

Would you like to play a musical instrument? Which one?

Reading the Text

See Introduction: Reading the Text, p.8.

Talking about the Story

Ask the children:

Can you remember what Mr Jones played? (trombone), Mrs Hum (drums), Mr Carr (guitar), Miss Toot (flute), Mr Middle (fiddle).

What did the cats and dogs do?

Would you like to live next door to Number 30 Rap Street?

Follow-up Activities

• Mime actions to the various instruments and see if the children can guess what instrument is being played.

• Play some pieces of music featuring a particular instrument (piano, drum, recorder). Let the children guess what is being played. You could also play a piece of music which has more than one instrument and see if the children can identify them.

• Say the rap:

Round the corner
Just in the next street
Lives a group of people
Who you'd like to meet.
It's a rap ...   it's a musical rap

They all make music
And they make it pretty loud.
Most people like it
And it makes them very proud.
It's a rap ... it's a musical rap.

But some people say,
"Stop that music, it's too loud
And such loud music
Shouldn't be allowed."
It's a rap ... it's a musical rap.

• Sing: "The big bass drum."

Oh! We can play on the big bass drum,
And this is the music to it.
Boom! boom! boom! goes the big bass drum
And that's the way we do it.

Act out playing the instrument at line three. Sing further verses fitting in different instruments, e.g. violin; triangle; tooty flute. You could also use school percussion instruments to play with the sounds in the third line.

145

Name_____

_____

In the queue

Ben   Jack   Mary   Ann

Who is first in the queue? _____

Who is fourth in the queue? _____

Who is third in the queue? _____

Who is second in the queue? _____

Answer the questions and colour the picture.

Moon Story

Moon Story

By Jillian Cutting
Illustrations by Jan van der Voo

Teaching Points for Set 4 Book 5:

sight words - there went
letter recognition - oo
focus - night-time

Moon Story

Introducing the Story

Before reading the story ask the children:

Have you seen a full moon in the sky?

Have you noticed that the moon is sometimes a different shape?

Have you ever travelled through the night?

Where were you going?

Did you stay awake?

The Oral Story-Telling

We were coming back from our holiday and Dad wanted to get home quickly so he drove all through the night. My little brother suddenly said, "Look, there is the moon!"

We went along the road and the moon climbed into the sky. It looked smaller but everywhere we went the moon seemed to follow. We went over the hills and the moon went over the hills. We went over the water and the moon went over the water. We went through the towns and the moon went through the towns. "The moon is following us," we said.

"Go to sleep!" said Mum. When we woke in the morning the sun was just beginning to shine but do you know what we could still see? We could see the moon.

Reading the Text

See Introduction: Reading the Text, p.8.

Talking about the Story

Ask the children:

Where did the moon follow the family? (hills, water, town)

What did Mum want the children to do?

What happened in the morning?

Follow-up Activities

• Talk to the children about the sky at night and how bright the moon can shine.

Talk about the first people to land on the moon. (Neil Armstrong and his pilot Edwin Aldrin landed on the moon in their lunar module "Eagle," on July 20, 1969.) What did they find? What was it like to walk on the moon? Would you like to go to the moon?

If possible show the children other books about the moon, e.g. "Spotlight: Moon" (Franklin Watts).

• Say the nursery rhyme:

The moon shines bright.
The stars give light.
You may play any game
At ten o'clock at night!

• Sing: "Hey diddle diddle".

• Give each child a copy of the photocopy master 35 (Activity Book B10).

First they should write the questions, then answer them with a 'yes' or a 'no'.

They can circle other items in the picture (flowers, duck, tractor) and colour the picture.

- Make a Moon Chart.

  Ask the children what they would like to take to the moon if they had to go there for a holiday.

  Write down all the suggestions on the board.

  Choose ten and help the children to write them on to their charts.

  Let them go and ask five friends what they would choose to take from the list but the friends can only choose five things. Put a tick on the chart for each thing the friends choose.

  Collect all the answers and show the children how to work out which was the most popular thing to take to the moon.

- Read to the class "Moon Game" by F. Asch (Picture Corgi).

Going to the Moon My friends will take…

	Mary	Bristi	Ben	Caleb	John
Teddy	✓	✓			
Tape		✓	✓		✓
Book		✓		✓	
Telescope	✓		✓	✓	✓
Lego	✓	✓		✓	✓
Toy car	✓	✓	✓	✓	✓
Cat	✓				
Best friend			✓		
T V			✓		✓
Sun hat				✓	

Dreams

Introducing the Story

Before reading the story ask the children:

Did you have a dream last night?

Was it a nice dream or was it a nightmare?

Did you tell anyone about your dream?

If you have a bad dream what do you do?

Reading the Text

See Introduction: Reading the Text, p.8.

Talking about the Story

Ask the children:

What did the little boy dream about?

What happened in his dream?

Would you have been frightened?

What did his Mum do?

Follow-up Activities

- Letter recognition (word building): 'oo'.

  Say the sound 'oon' to the children and let them make it too.

  Tell them you are going to give them some sounds to build up a word.

  Ask the children what word you are making if you add 'm' to 'oon'; 's' to 'oon'; 'sp' to 'oon'.

  Ask the children what word you are making if you add 't' to 'oot'; 'b' to 'oot'; 'h' to 'oot'; 'r' to 'oot'.

  Ask the children what word you are making if you add 'f' to 'ool'; 't' to 'ool'; 'p' to 'ool'.

- Riddle: "What am I dreaming about?"

  It is a big animal.
  It has a long spiky tail.
  It can breathe fire.
  It is a .....

  He's a very big person.
  He's very, very strong.
  You find him in story books.
  He must be a .....

  She is very small.
  She has delicate wings.
  She has a magic wand.
  She must be a ....

- Read to the class, "One night at a time" by Susan Hill (Hamish Hamilton).

- Read to the class, "One Moonlit Night" by R. and D. Armitage (Picture Puffin).

Sunflowers

Introduction to the Story

Before reading the story ask the children:

Have you ever grown any seeds?

What did you have to do?

What did you grow?

Did it take a long time to grow?

Reading the Text

See Introduction: Reading the Text, p.8.

Talking about the Story

Ask the children;

What did the farmer plant?

What did the seeds need in order to grow?

Did you guess what was growing?

What do you think the farmer will do with the sunflowers?

Follow-up Activities

• Grow some different seeds with the children.

CRESS You need cress seeds, water and damp paper. (blotting paper or several pieces of kitchen roll)

Wet the paper thoroughly and sprinkle on the seeds. Do not let the paper dry out.

You can write a letter with the seeds.

BEANS You need bean seeds, a jam jar and blotting paper or kitchen roll.

Line the jar with the blotting paper.

Place the bean seeds between the paper and the jar.

Fill the jar 1/3 full with water.

SUNFLOWER You need a small pot about 10 cms deep.

Fill the pot with fine soil. Dampen the soil.

Put in one sunflower seed.

Plant outside after plant reaches 10 cms.

• Say the poem:

A little seed
For me to sow...
A little earth
To make it grow...
A little hole
A little pat...
A little wish
And that is that.
A little sun
A little shower
A little while
And then - a flower! Mabel Watts.

• Say the nursery rhyme:

Mary, Mary,
Quite contrary,
How does your garden grow?
With silver bells,
And cockle shells,
And pretty maids all in a row.

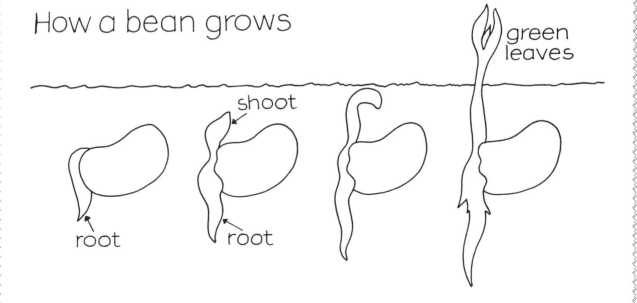

How a bean grows

green leaves

shoot

root

root

149

 **35** Name_____

_____

What can you find?

yes or no

Is there a 🌙 ?   _____

Is there a ?   _____

Is there a 🐱 ?   _____

___ ___ ___ 🐴 ?   _____

___ ___ ___ ⭐ ?   _____

___ ___ ___ 🌳 ?   _____

What else can you find?

Write the sentences and answer the questions.
Put a circle around what else is found. Colour the picture.

The Babysitters

The Babysitters
By Joy Cowley
Illustrations by Val Biro

Teaching Points for Set 4 Book 6:	sight words - after looked letter recognition - cr focus - story endings

The Babysitters

Introducing the Story

Before reading the story ask the children:

Do you have a babysitter sometimes?

Are you always good when the babysitter comes?

Are you allowed to stay up a little later when the babysitter comes?

The Oral Story-Telling

Mrs Crocodile was going out. She left baby crocodile with her friends but before she left she said to him, "I want you to behave yourself while I'm out. And don't Snip-snap at the babysitter. Remember, **no Snip-snap!**" First the giraffe looked after baby crocodile but do you know what he did? Yes, Snip-snap! Then the hippo looked after him but do you know what he did? More Snip-snap. Then the tiger looked after him but do you know what he did? Again, Snip-snap! Then the monkey looked after him. Monkey had a good idea to stop the Snip-snap! Do you know what he did? He took baby crocodile's ribbon and tied it round the baby crocodile's jaws! Now there was no Snip-snap!

Reading the Text

See Introduction: Reading the Text, p.8.

Talking about the Story

Ask the children:

Who looked after baby crocodile?

Did they like looking after him?

What do you think Mrs. Crocodile said when she saw what monkey had done to baby crocodile?

Did you think it was a good idea?

Follow-up Activities

• Give a copy of the photocopy master 36 (Activity Book B11) to each child and ask the children to fill in the missing words. They can write their own words in the speech bubble.

• Letter recognition: 'cr', 'ch'.

Draw two columns on the board.

Write at the top of one the letters 'cr' and at the top of the other the letters 'ch'.

Divide the children into teams giving each team a different coloured piece of chalk. Tell them you are going to give each child a word and they must listen very carefully and then tick the column that they think the word begins with.

Offer some of the following words: crumb, cracker, cradle, crane, crash, crawl, crayon, cream, creature, crocodile;

church, chain, chimp, chocolate, child, chalk, change, cheap, cheese, chimney, chips. The team which gets the most words correct wins.

• Sing or say the song:

Mrs Giraffe looked after the baby
She cuddled him on her lap.
She sang him a song that didn't take long
But the crocodile went "Snip-snap!"

Mr Hippo looked after the baby, etc.
Miss Tiger looked after the baby, etc.

Little Monkey looked after the baby.
She tied his jaw with some string.
She sang him a song that didn't take long
But the crocodile said not a thing!

- Read to the class, "Mr and Mrs Pig's Evening Out" by Mary Rayner (Piccolo).

The Knight and the Dragon

Introducing the Story

Before reading the story ask the children:

What animal does a knight try to catch?

Where do you think he might find a dragon?

What clothes do you think a knight should wear?

What will the dragon try to do to the knight?

Reading the Text

See Introduction: Reading the Text, p.8.

Talking about the Story

Ask the children:

Can you remember who the knight asked about the dragon?

Look at the picture on page 14 and 15. How do you know the dragon is near?

Why did the bird laugh at the knight?

Follow-up Activities

- Talk to the children about 'funny endings'. Did they guess what these first two stories would finish with? Did they think they were good endings? Did they make them laugh? Do they know any other stories like these with funny endings?

- Play: "Hunt the dragon". (a version of "Hunt the thimble")

Draw a small dragon on to a piece of paper and hide it somewhere in the classroom.

Tell the children to guess where he is hiding and you will give them help. If they are near you will say, "Yes. You can feel the dragon's hot breath." If they are in the wrong place you will say "No. The dragon is not near here." When they have discovered him perhaps the person who found him would like to hide him.

- Make a book about dragons.

Talk to the children about all the things they know about dragons and write them down. Show the children how to group things together, e.g. What they think dragons eat, where they live, what they do, stories they know about dragons.

Help the children decide how to put all this into a book for the rest of the class.

What pictures do they need to provide? (Some of these could be photocopied or cut out. They do not always need to be drawn.) Will they provide a contents list?

Write out simple sentences for them to put into their book or to copy into the book.

Finally make a cover and decide upon a title and cover design. Put on the authors' and illustrators' names.

- Read to the class the story, "The Knight and the Dragon" by Tomie de Paola (Magnet).

- Read to the class the story, "There's no such thing as a dragon" by Jack Kent (Picture Puffin).

Pirate Pete's Treasure

Introducing the Story

Before reading the story ask the children:

What do you think pirates keep in their treasure chests?

Where do they get the treasure from?

Where do they hide the treasure?

Reading the Text

See Introduction: Reading the Text, p.8.

Talking about the Story

Ask the children:

What should Pete have done so that he could find his treasure?

What did he do when he couldn't find it?

Do you feel sorry for him?

Follow-up Activities

• Game: "Find the treasure".

Draw a simple grid on the board, e.g. six letters in columns across and six numbers down the side.

Choose a square and write it down on a piece of paper. Tell the children you have hidden the treasure in the square you have written down. Can they find it? Let the children take it in turns to select a square. They must tell you the grid reference and then mark it off by putting a cross over it. The child who finds the treasure could then choose another square and write down his or her hiding place.

• Our Pirate Map.

Let the children make a pirate map by working in pairs. Include such suggestions as: shark reef, black rock, skeleton cave, wild woods, dead man's cove, eagle's lair.

To make the map look more authentic it is possible to singe the edges carefully.

• Read to the class, "The man whose mother was a Pirate" by Margaret Mahy (Puffin).

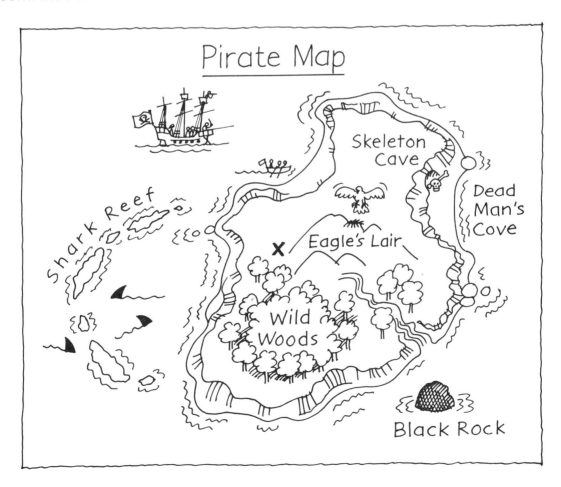

153

Fill in the words

The  looked after the
"Snip Snap."

The _____ ____ the
" _____ "
____ ____ .

The  _____ ____ the
" _____ "
____ ____ .

The  _____ ____ the
" _____ "
____ ____ .

What did baby say to Mum?

Fill in the missing words. Make up a sentence for what
baby said to Mum when she came back.

The Whale

The Whale
By Jill Eggleton
Illustrations by Jan van der Voo

Teaching Points for Set 4 Book 7:

sight words - we will
letter recognition - wh
focus - silent letters

The Whale

Introducing the Story

Before reading the story ask the children:

Where do whales live?

Do you think that they have to live in the sea?

What might happen if they got washed up on the shore?

The Oral Story-Telling

One day we were all playing on the beach. My dad was sunbathing on a rug. The tide was just starting to come in over the sand. Then, what do you think came in with the tide? A big whale! It had been swimming in the shallow water and when a big wave came up the sand the poor whale was dragged in with it.

The waves pulled back into the sea but the whale could not go out.

"We will help the whale," said Dad. "Get buckets of water!" What do you think we did with the buckets of water? We poured the water on the whale. The sun got hotter and hotter. What could we do to keep the whale cool? We got buckets and buckets of water to put on the whale.

At last the tide came in again. It came over the sand and it went under the whale. At last the whale was able to float again. "Push!" said Dad. We pushed the whale into the sea and it swam away. All our hard work had saved the whale.

Reading the Text

See Introduction: Reading the Text, p.8.

Talking about the Story

Ask the children:

What did Dad do to save the whale?

How did the whale get back into the sea?

Do you think that the whale was frightened of the family or was the family frightened of the whale?

Follow-up Activities

• Write on the blackboard the letters 'wh'. Say the sound for the children and explain that although there are two letters they only make one sound. Explain that we call the letter that we do not sound a silent letter. This sound starts lots of words that ask questions - What? Where? When? Why? Ask the children some questions: "What is your name?" "Where do you live?" "When is your birthday?" "Why do you wear a coat in the winter?"

Encourage the children to ask you questions starting with the 'wh' sound.

• Give each child a copy of the photocopy master 37 (Activity Book B12).

Ask the children to make words using 'wh', then to write them out.

Then they can colour the whale and give it a name.

• Say the rhyme:

We had to save the whale
To push it back into the sea.
It might not live if it stayed on the sand
And we wanted to let it go free.

We poured lots of buckets of water
We poured them to keep the whale wet.
We knew that if his skin dried out
He couldn't be saved by a vet.

At last the tide came rushing in
And the whale had the chance to go free.
We all pushed together to help the whale
To live once again in the sea.

- In the school playground pace out and mark with chalk how long a whale is. (Blue whales can grow to more than 33 metres.)
- Tell the children the story, "Amos and Boris" by William Steig (Picture Lions).

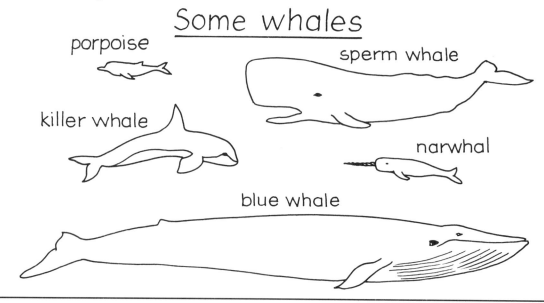

Some whales

porpoise

sperm whale

killer whale

narwhal

blue whale

The Pie

Introducing the Story

Before reading the story ask the children:

Do you like to eat fruit pie or fruit tarts?

What fruit do you like best in a pie?

Do you know what pastry is made of?

Have you baked a pie or tarts?

Reading the Text

See Introduction: Reading the Text, p.8.

Talking about the Story

Ask the children:

What did the first cook put in his pie?

What did the second cook put in her pie?

Who did they give their pies to?

What did the third cook put in his pie?

Who ate that pie?

Follow-up Activities

- Sing the Nursery Rhyme: "Simple Simon".

Simple Simon met a pieman
Going to the fair.

Said Simple Simon to the pieman
"Let me taste your ware."

Said the pieman to Simple Simon,
"Show me first your penny."
Said Simple Simon to the pieman,
"Indeed I have not any."

- Say the rhyme:

The first cook made a pie
He made it nice and sweet.
He gave it to the king and said,
"Have this for a treat."

The second cook made a pie
She made it nice and sweet.
She gave it to the king and said,
"Have this for a treat."

The third cook made a pie
Saying, "I hope no-one looks.
We won't give it to the king," she said,
This pie is for the cooks!"

- Make jam tarts to take home.

The Hen

Introducing the Story

Before reading the story ask the children:

Where do eggs come from?

Do you like to eat eggs? How do you like them?

What do we call a hen if it is eaten as meat?

Do you like chicken? Do you like any other meat?

Reading the Text

See Introduction: Reading the Text, p.8.

Talking about the Story

Ask the children:

Why did the hen not want to lay eggs?

What was the farmer going to do?

What did the hen say?

What did the hen do?

Follow-up Activities

• Say the Nursery Rhyme:

Hickety pickety my black hen,
She lays eggs for gentlemen.
Sometimes nine and sometimes ten,
Hickety pickety, my black hen.

• Say the rhyme: "How many eggs?"

One clucking hen
Sitting on the straw
Laid one brown egg
And then one more.
How many eggs?

Two clucking hens
Sitting on the straw
Laid two brown eggs
And then one more.
How many eggs?

Three clucking hens
Sitting on the straw
Laid three brown eggs
And then one more.
How many eggs?

• Decorate eggs.

Boil the eggs then paint the shell or draw on them with felt tip pens.
You can add food colouring to the water in which you boil them to give an overall colour.

• Talk with the children about different ways of eating eggs:
boiled - hard or soft; fried; scrambled; poached; omelette.

• Read to the children, "The Sly Fox and the Little Red Hen" (Ladybird).

• Read "Cluck Cluck" by Patricia Casey (Walker Books). As this story is mostly the sound effects that the farm animals make, the children might like to share the reading of this text.

• Read with the class, "Rosie's Walk" by Pat Hutchins (Picture Puffin).

37

Name_____

_____

Make some wh words

__at   __ __y   __ __ere

__ __ale   __ __ile   __ __en

__ __ich   __ __eel   __ __o

__ __ose

Now write the wh words

____ ____ ____ ____

____ ____ ____ ____

Grandpa's New Car

Grandpa's New Car

By Jill Eggleton
Illustrations by Terry Burton

Teaching Points for Set 4 Book 8:

sight words - come had took
letter recognition - sl tr
focus - sentences

Grandpa's New Car

Introducing the Story

Before reading the story ask the children:

Have you ever watched anyone working on a car?

How would you mend a flat tyre?

What else can break down on a car?

The Oral Story-Telling

One day Grandma looked at their old car. The tyres were flat, the lights were broken and the number plate had fallen off. "I want a new car," said Grandma. "We don't need to buy one," said Grandpa, "I'll make a new car."

He took the wheels off the truck and he took the seat off the truck. He took the motor out of the truck. He built a new car.

"I have made a new car," said Grandpa. "Come for a ride, Grandma!" Grandma got in the new car. The wheels bumped along and the engine made a funny noise.

"Where are we going?" asked Grandma. "We're going to get a new truck," said Grandpa.

Reading the Story

See Introduction: Reading the Text, p.8.

Talking about the Story

Ask the children:

What did Grandpa take from the truck to make the new car? (wheels, seats, motor)

Did you think that the car Grandpa built would be good?

What kind of new truck do you think they chose?

Follow-up Activities

• Sing with the children: "The wheels on the truck go round and round."

The wheels on the truck go round and round,
Round and round, round and round.
The wheels on the truck go round and round
All day long.

The wipers on the truck go back and forth, etc.
The trucks on the road go up and down, etc.
The drivers in the trucks all sing a song, etc.

• Give each child a copy of the photocopy master 38 (Activity Book B13). Ask the children to build as many words as they can to make a wall of words. The letters in the wheelbarrow can be used with some of the bricks.

• Use Lego or Sticklebricks to build a car.

• Pass the word: The 'tr' sound.

Ask the children to sit in a group and to take it in turns to think of 'tr' words. The teacher can prompt by giving children sentences in which words starting with 'tr' occur. (train, truck, trip, trap, treat, treasure)

The Pirate Chief

Introducing the Story

Before reading the story ask the children:

What did pirates do?

What did they wear?

Were they good people or bad people?

Reading the Text

See Introduction: Reading the Text, p.8.

Talking about the Story

Ask the children:

Can you remember what Pirate One was going to do on board ship? (clean the ship) Pirate Two? (make the beds) Pirate Three? (cook the dinners)

What was the pirate chief going to do?

Follow-up Activities

• Say the Rhyme: "The Bold Pirates".

Five bold pirates
Heard a lion roar.
One was frightened
And that left four.

Four bold pirates
Sailing on the sea.
One was eaten by a shark
And that left three.

Three bold pirates
Wondering what to do.
One fell overboard
And that left two.

Two bold pirates
Lying in the sun.
One had to walk the plank
And that left one.

One bold pirate
Resting in the sun.
A seagull pecked his nose
And then there were none.

• Pass the word: The 'sl' sound.

Ask the children to sit in a group and take it in turns to think of 'sl' words. (The teacher can give a clue if a child is stuck, e.g. A snail moves ....., not fast. It feels moist and .....

• Read with the children, "One-Eyed Jake" by Pat Hutchins (Picture Puffin).

The Jolly Roger

Monkey and Elephant

Introducing the Story

Before reading the story ask the children:

Do you like to play when it's your bedtime?

Do you like to sleep in the daytime or night-time?

Can you remember any creatures that are awake at night? (hamsters, owls, hedgehogs)

What do we call animals which only come out at night? (nocturnal)

Reading the Text

See Introduction: Reading the Text, p.8.

Talking about the Story

Ask the children:

Who liked to sleep in the day and play at night?

What do you think monkey did when elephant woke him up in the daytime?

Follow-up Activities

• Sing the song: "The animal fair".

I went to the animal fair.
The birds and the beasts were there.
The big baboon by the light of the moon
Was combing his golden hair.
The monkey fell out of his bunk
And fell down the elephant's trunk.
The elephant sneezed and fell on his knees
And what became of the monk-ey monk-ey
Monk-ey monk-ey monk-ey?

• A Rhyming game.

Ask the children to listen and then complete the rhyming sentences:

The monkey had a cup of tea.

The monkey saw a buzzing .....

The monkey ate a green .....

The monkey climbed a tall .....

The monkey sailed out to .....

• Read to the children, "Goodnight Owl" by Pat Hutchins (Picture Puffin).

Nocturnal Animals

38

Name_____

Build the wall

ome	ome	ome

ad	ad	ad	ad

ing	ing	ing

ook	ook	ook	ook

Use the letters in the wheelbarrow to make the words.

The Magic Tree

The Magic Tree
By Jill Eggleton
Illustrations by Peter Stevenson

Teaching Points for Set 4 Book 9:

sight words - eat want
letter recognition - tr
focus - growth and change

The Magic Tree

Introducing the Story

Before reading the story ask the children:

Can you remember what seeds need to make them grow? (soil, rain, sun)

What colour do you think seeds are?

Do you think that a blue and yellow seed would produce an ordinary plant?

Can you think of any names for magic people? (elf, gnome, leprechaun, pixie, fairy)

The Oral Story-Telling

Can you remember how we had to water our seeds and put them in a sunny place in the classroom? Well I know of a little person who could do magic and he could command the rain to rain and the sun to shine and he grew a very special plant indeed. The magic man planted a very unusual seed. It was blue and yellow. He looked up at the sky. "Rain!" he said. "Come down!" A big black cloud appeared in the sky. It grew bigger and bigger and it covered the sun. In a moment rain came down and the blue and yellow seed grew. Then the magic man looked up at the sky. "Sun!" he said "Come out!" At once the black cloud disappeared and the sun came out and the seed grew. It grew into a tree. Guess what colour its leaves were? (blue) Guess what colour its branches were? (yellow) But can you guess what grew on the magic tree? It wasn't fruit and it wasn't seeds. It was - jellybeans!

Reading the Text

See Introduction: Reading the Text, p.8.

Talking about the Story

Ask the children:

What colour was the seed the magic man planted?

What did the magic man say to the rain?

What did he say to the sun?

What was funny about the tree? (blue leaves and yellow branches)

What grew on the magic tree?

Follow-up Activities

• Say the rhyme:

The magic man planted a blue and yellow seed.
What was going to grow?
He had a secret plan in mind
As he put that seed in a row.

Magic man looked up into the sky.
"Come down, rain," he said.
And down came the rain in big wet drops
And they fell on magic man's head.

The magic man looked up to the sky
"Come out, sun," he said.
And out came the sun all bright and warm
And shone on magic man's head.

Then the seed grew into a tree
With branches yellow and blue.
And something was growing on the tree.
I wonder if you knew?

Jellybeans grew upon that tree
Jellybeans red, blue and pink.
If I planted a blue and yellow seed,
Would I get jellybeans, do you think?

- Ask the children if they can remember the story of "Jack and the Beanstalk". Can they tell it to you?
- Say some tongue-twisters using 'tr', e.g. - The truck tried to travel on the track.

Tricky tractors try to trample trees.

Ask the children if they can hear the sound 'tr' that starts most of those words. See if they can think of other words that start with 'tr'. It might be necessary to give them clues to the words. Some words are: trace, traffic, trail, trampoline, trap, travel, treasure, tricycle, trip.

The Bird and the Caterpillar

Introducing the Story

Before reading the story ask the children:

Do you think a bird would be friendly with a caterpillar?

What might the bird want to do to the caterpillar?

Do you know what happens to caterpillars after some time?

Reading the Text

See Introduction: Reading the Text, p.8.

Talking about the Story

Ask the children:

Did you notice that the caterpillar was getting bigger and bigger?

Why do you think it was getting bigger?

What did the caterpillar say to stop the bird from eating him?

Follow-up Activities

- Share with the children, the book, "Keeping Minibeasts: Caterpillars" (Franklin Watts).

- Give each child a copy of the photocopy master 39 (Activity Book B14). Ask the children to connect the two pictures on each line by writing the sentence, "I want to eat you". The first sentence is written out as an example for the children. When they have finished the children can draw a line to connect the two items together, e.g. bird with worm, girl with fish and chips.

- Sing the rhyme:

Little Arabella Miller
Found a woolly caterpillar.
First it crawled upon her mother,
Then upon her baby brother;
All said, "Arabella Miller,
Take away that caterpillar."

- Read with the class, "The Very Hungry Caterpillar" by Eric Carle (Picture Puffin).

- Read the children, "The Bad-Tempered Ladybird" by Eric Carle (Picture Puffin).

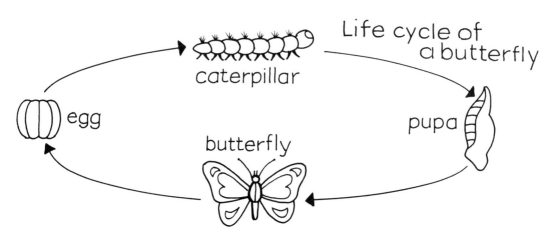

Life cycle of a butterfly

caterpillar

egg

pupa

butterfly

Keep Looking!

Introducing the Story

Before reading the story ask the children:

Have you ever lost anything?

Did you find it in the end?

Is there anyone in your house who often loses things?

Do your Mum or Dad say anything to you if you can't find something? Do they say, "Don't ask me." "It's where you left it." "If you put your things in the proper place you would not lose them."?

Reading the Text

See Introduction: Reading the Text, p.8.

Talking about the Story

Ask the children:

Can you remember what Mum lost? (keys, glasses, slippers)

What did Dad keep saying?

Did you notice that Dad had put on Mum's slippers?

Do you like to play tricks on people like that?

Follow-up Activities

• Say the chant:

Mum had lost her car keys
She couldn't see them anywhere.
She looked in the kitchen
And her keys were there.

Mum had lost her glasses
She couldn't see them anywhere.
She looked in the bedroom
And her glasses were there.

Mum had lost her slippers
Dad sat in the comfy seat.
He just said "Keep looking."
But he had them on his feet!

• Play: "Hunt the thimble".

Hide a small object in the classroom. As the children search give them clues, e.g. "You are getting warmer." "Now you're very cold."

• The lost letter.

Tell the children that you are going to say some words which have lost a letter. They are to say which letter or sound has been lost, e.g. farm arm. Which letter is lost?

Some words to use: hedge, edge; hand, and; cat, at; table, able; gate, ate; plate, late; bring, ring; peach, each; blow, low; pin, in; cup, up; train, rain; bus, us; gold, old.

• Read to the children, "Tricky Tortoise" by Adrienne Kennaway (Picture Knight).

39

Name_____

_____

Who eats what?

 I want to eat you

 I want to eat you

 — — — — — — — — —

 — — — — — — — — —

 — — — — — — — — —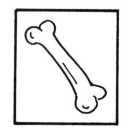

Write the sentences and draw a line to show who eats what.

I Like Worms!

By Joy Cowley
Illustrations by Astrid Matijasevic

Teaching Points for Set 4 Book 10:	sight words - likes play to letter recognition - fr focus - the seasons

I Like Worms!

Introducing the Story

Before reading the story ask the children:

Where would you expect to find worms?

What colour do you think worms are?

Would you like to eat worms?

What creatures do eat worms?

The Oral Story-Telling

Mrs Henrietta Hen lifted down her cookery book. "Now, how shall I eat my favourite food today?" Can you guess what her favourite food is? It is worms. Mrs Hen says, "I like big worms and I like fat worms and I like pink worms and I like purple worms. I like worms for lunch and worms for tea. I like little worms and skinny worms and red worms and orange worms. I think that worms are good for me! I like worms in my soup and I like worms in my pies. I also like worms on my pizza and I like worms and fries. I like worms in a bowl or worms in a jug. I like worms in a jar and I like worms in a mug. Most of all **I like worms**!" And Mrs Henrietta Hen decided to have worm stew for lunch and worms and custard for pudding.

Reading the Text

See Introduction: Reading the Text, p.8.

Talking about the Story

Ask the children:

Can you remember some of the ways Mrs Hen liked to eat worms?

Do you think that we eat any food that looks a bit like worms? (spaghetti)

Have you ever seen a bird trying to pull a worm out of the ground? Who won?

Follow-up Activities

• Share with the children the photographs and the text in "Keeping Minibeasts: Earthworms" (Franklin Watts).

• Say the rhyme with hand actions:

   Under a stone where the earth was firm,
   I found a wriggly, wriggly worm;
   (Use one forefinger for the worm;
   partially cover with the other hand.)
   "Good morning," I said.
   "How are you today?"
   (Uncover the forefinger.)
   But the wriggly worm just wriggled away!
   (Wriggle forefinger away up the other arm.)

• Tracking game: "Find the 'fr'".

   Give the children a page of a newspaper or magazine and ask them to mark in highlighter pen every time they see 'fr' at the start of a word.

The Little Bird

Introducing the Story

Before reading the story ask the children:

Where do we usually see birds?

Have you ever seen a bird in a cage? Was it a big cage or a small cage?

Do you think that all types of birds would be happy in cages?

Do you know anyone who has a bird in a cage? (budgerigar, canary, zebra finch)

What kinds of birds might you find in cages?

Reading the Text

See Introduction: Reading the Text, p.8.

Talking about the Story

Ask the children:

Why do you think that the little garden bird did not sing in the cage?

Do you think that the little girl was kind to the bird?

What did she give the bird to make it happy?

What did make the bird happy?

Follow-up Activities

- Say the following finger rhyme for children to learn. Use four fingers on the right hand for berries and use the left hand for the blackbird.

Four scarlet berries
Left upon a tree.
"Thanks," said the blackbird,
"These will do for me."
He ate numbers one and two,
Then ate number three.
When he'd eaten number four,
There was none to see!

- Share with the children, "Topsy and Tim can help birds" by Jean and Gareth Adamson (Blackie)- an activity book with ideas about looking after garden birds.

- Make a chart of different common garden birds, e.g. blackbird, starling, blue tit, robin, sparrow, etc. Tell the children to place a tick in the relevant column if they see one of the birds. It would be useful to have a reference book for children to check which bird they have seen, e.g. "Birds" by Henry Pluckrose (Hamish Hamilton).

Garden birds What have we seen?	
Blackbird	
Starling	
Blue Tit	
Robin	
Sparrow	
Pigeon	
Thrush	
Put a tick next to each kind of bird as you have seen it.	

Our Dog, Skunk

Introducing the Story

Before reading the story ask the children:

Do you have a pet dog? What is its name?

Do you think dogs like to run and catch sticks?

What else do you think dogs like to play?

Reading the Text

See Introduction: Reading the Text, p.8.

Talking about the Story

Ask the children:

Can you remember where Skunk liked to play in Spring? Summer? Autumn? Winter?

Why do you think she is called Skunk?

Do you think Skunk liked to have a bath?

Follow-up Activities

• Give each child a copy of the photocopy master 40 (Activity Book B15). When the child has copied the words to write on each line, he or she can join Skunk to the right activity for the season.

• Say the rhyme:

I know a very little dog
Whose coat is covered in dots.
He likes to play in the garden
And so we call him Spots.

I know another little dog
Whose coat is red and rusty.
He trails his ears along the ground
And so we call him Dusty.

I know a very big dog
He likes to run and catch.
He has a brown mark across one eye
And so we call him Patch.

• Talk about how to look after dogs. They need proper food and lots of exercise and grooming. Look at pictures of different kinds of dogs and discuss which kinds need more attention than others and in what ways.

• Read "What-a-Mess in Spring/Summer/Autumn/Winter" by Frank Muir (Benn).

Different dogs need different kinds of care

Collie

Greyhound

Foxhound

Pekingese

Name_____

What does Skunk like to do?

In spring   likes to play

in the

In summer   __ __ __ __

__ __ __

In autumn   __ __ __ __

__ __ __

In winter   __ __ __ __

__ __

Write the sentences and draw a line to show what
Skunk likes to do each season.

Sunshine Spirals Set 1 Running Record Sheet

The Big Race

Set 1 Book 6

Name .... Class .... Date ....

	Omission	Told	Sounds	Self-correct
The big race.				
I ride in the big race.				
I climb in the big race.				
I paddle in the big race.				
I swim in the big race.				
I run in the big race.				
I win the big race!				
TOTALS				

Questions:

Can you remember the races the girl was in?

Which race would you have liked to do?

How do you think the girl felt when she won the race?

Analysis and Future Action:

Where is My Hat?

Set 1 Book 7

Name .... Class .... Date ....

	Omission	Told	Sounds	Self-Correct
Here is a red sock.				
Here is a red shoe.				
Here is a blue sock.				
Here is a blue shoe.				
Here is a green tie.				
Where is my hat?				
On the monkey!				
TOTALS				

Questions:

Can you remember what the clown found when he was looking for his hat?

Who had the clown's hat all the time?

What do you think the clown said when he found his hat?

Analysis and Future Action:

Sunshine Spirals Set 2 Running Record Sheet

		Omission	Told	Sounds	Self-correct
Name .... Class .... Date					
Set 2 **Book 2**					
Elephant Walk					
Questions:	The elephant went for a walk.				
What shops did the elephant go into?	The elephant went into the toy shop.				
What did the children do with the elephant?	The elephant went into the sports shop.				
Why do you think the elephant wanted to go for a walk?	It went into the dress shop.				
Which place do you think the elephant liked most?	The elephant went into the book shop.				
Analysis and Future Action:	It went into the school.				
	The children took the elephant home.				
		TOTALS			

		Omission	Told	Sounds	Self-Correct
Name .... Class .... Date					
Set 2 **Book 5**					
I Can Climb	"I can climb the tree," said the monkey.				
Questions:	"I can climb the tree," said the snake.				
Which animals do you think climbed the tree quickly?	"I can climb the tree," said the leopard.				
Which animals do you think climbed the tree slowly?	"I can climb the tree," said the spider.				
Who should not have climbed the tree?	"I can climb the tree," said the ant.				
Would you have climbed the tree?	"I can climb the tree," said the elephant.				
Analysis and Future Action:	Crash!				
		TOTALS			

Sunshine Spirals Set 3 Running Record Sheet

Name .... Class .... Date ....

	Omission	Told	Sounds	Self-correct

Jack and the Giant

Set 3 Book 1

	Jack went to the giant's house.
	He went up the giant's path.
	He went up the giant's steps.
	He went under the giant's door.
	"I am cold," said Jack. "I want a hot bath."
	The giant came in.
	"Get out of my soup!"

Questions:

How did Jack get to the giant's house?

What did Jack do to get warm?

What do you think happened when the giant saw Jack?

Analysis and Future Action:

TOTALS

Name .... Class .... Date ....

	Omission	Told	Sounds	Self-Correct

The Penguins

Set 3 Book 4

	The penguins walk on the ice.
	They slide on the ice.
	The penguins dive into the water. They look for fish to eat.
	The killer whales come.
	The killer whales look for penguins to eat!
	The penguins swim. The penguins swim faster and faster.
	The penguins jump on to the ice. They are safe!

Questions:

What did the penguins do on the ice?

Why did the penguins go into the sea?

Why do you think the whale was after the penguins?

What do you think happened next?

Analysis and Future Action:

TOTALS

Sunshine Spirals Set 4 Running Record Sheet

Name ....Class ....Date ....

Set 4
Book 5

Moon Story

Questions:

Where did the moon follow the car?

What did Mum want the children to do?

Why do you think it looked as though the moon was following the car?

Analysis and Future Action:

	Omission	Told	Sounds	Self-correct
"Look! There is the moon!"				
The moon climbed into the sky. It got smaller and smaller.				
We went over the hills. The moon went over the hills.				
We went over the water. The moon went over the water.				
We went through the towns. The moon went through the towns.				
"The moon is following us," we said. "Go to sleep!" said Mum.				
In the morning, Dad said, "Look! There is the moon! It followed us all night."				
TOTALS				

Name ....Class ....Date ....

Set 4
Book 9

The Magic Tree

Questions:

What did the man need to make the seed grow?

What happened to the seed?

How do you know the tree was magic?

What magic tree would you like to plant?

Analysis and Future Action:

	Omission	Told	Sounds	Self-Correct
The magic man planted a seed. It was blue and yellow.				
He looked up at the sky. "Rain!" he said. "Come down! Come down!"				
The rain came down and the seed grew.				
The magic man looked up at the sky. "Sun!" he said. "Come out! Come out!"				
The sun came out and the seed grew.				
The seed grew into a tree. It had blue leaves and yellow branches.				
The magic man looked at the tree. "Jellybeans!" he said. "I have a jellybean tree."				
TOTALS				

Letter sound/letter name record

Name...Class................................Date.............................

	a	b	c	d	e	f	g	h	i	j	k	l	m	n	o	p	qu	r	s	t	u	v	w	x	y	z	(x)
Knows sound																											
Knows name																											
Can form correctly																											

Word recognition record

a	at	away	big	can	down	going	had	he	help	here	
are	in	into	is	it	look	me	my	no	not	on	over
his	some	the	this	to	under	want	we	went	will	with	you
said											

Check off each letter/word as the child masters it.

Sunshine Spirals Sets 1 to 4
Letter blend record

Name .... Class .... Date ....

Knows sound	bl	ch	cl	cr	fr	oo	pl	sh	sk	sl	sp	st	sw	th	tr	wh

Word recognition record

a	after	and	are	away	big	can	
come	did	down	eat	fast	from	get	go
going	had	have	he	help	here	his	I
in	into	is	it	likes	little	look	looked
makes	me	my	no	not	of	on	out
over	past	play	put	said	see	some	the
there	they	this	to	too	took	under	up
want	we	went	what	will	with	you	your

Check off each letter blend/word as the child masters it.